Sir Cyril

MY LIFE AS A SOCIAL
ENTREPRENEUR

CYRIL TAYLOR

FOREWORD BY LORD ADONIS
INTRODUCTION BY PETER WILBY
EDITED BY CONOR RYAN

AMBERLEY

This book is dedicated to all those in the world who wish to do good and to help others

ACKNOWLEDGEMENTS

I am most grateful to the following people, without whose help I would not have been able to publish this book:

Lord Adonis for the Foreword

Peter Wilby for the Introduction

Conor Ryan for editing the book

Hannelore Fuller for turning my poor handwriting into a typed version of the book and Debbie Wilson for stepping into the breach

Jonathan Reeve, the Editorial Director of Amberley Publishing for publishing the book

First published 2013

Amberley Publishing
The Hill, Stroud
Gloucestershire, GL5 4EP
www.amberley-books.com

British Library Cataloguing in Publication Data.
A catalogue record for this book is available from the British Library.

ISBN 978 1 4456 1192 1 print
ISBN 978 1 4456 1199 0 ebook

Typesetting and Origination by Amberley Publishing
Printed in the UK.

CONTENTS

INTRODUCTION BY
PETER WILBY

'We are going to what was,' said Sir Cyril Taylor, 'the worst school in the country, on every possible measure.' It was 2006 and we were travelling by taxi through a South London housing estate of rusting vans, peeling paint and – this being football World Cup time – St George's flags hanging from almost every other front window. Our destination was the former Malory School, where the proportion of pupils acquiring five A*–C grades at GCSE consistently fell below 20 per cent and, in some years, below 10 per cent. Now, under New Labour's academies programme, it had recently been re-branded and linked in a federation with Haberdashers' Aske's, already a city academy and, according to Sir Cyril, 'the most over-subscribed school in the country'. These were not the only schools I would hear him describe, with characteristic over-statement, as 'worst in the country' or 'most over-subscribed'. But Sir Cyril, then chairman of the Specialist Schools and Academies Trust, was a man with a mission, who brooked little argument.

On arrival at the Haberdashers' Aske's Knights Academy, as it was by then called, Sir Cyril bounded from the taxi (at seventy-one, he could still somehow bound despite a gammy knee) to meet the new principal, who was waiting at the door. 'What proportion of these children are on free school meals?' Sir Cyril asked almost immediately.

Further questions came thick and fast as we met a group of senior staff. 'Can we possibly change the cycle that was going down and down here?' (A rhetorical question if ever there was one.) 'How do you measure ethos? Could you keep a diary or something? Do you have supervised silent reading? How many books will you have?' A teacher mentioned electronic materials. 'There is increasing evidence you need books,' said Taylor sharply. He has always been very hot on evidence. 'What is the cost of the new building?' £26 million. 'So why is it listed as £38 million?' That was catch-up maintenance. 'That ought to be specified.' Sir Cyril has always been hot on money, too.

The overall effect was a curious mixture of a chief executive visiting an outpost of his corporate empire and a scoutmaster rallying boys for an arduous cross-country hike. 'You are blue-sky thinkers,' he told the senior staff. They looked suitably impressed, if slightly daunted.

I had then known Sir Cyril Taylor for twenty years, but this was the first time I had seen him, as it were, in action. As a recent *New Statesman* editor, I was not then (and, despite Sir Cyril's untiring efforts, am not now) a natural supporter of academies. My position on them is best described as agnostic, allied to a certain weariness with endless arguments about who governs schools and what we should call them. But of Sir Cyril's sincerity, enthusiasm and determination to get what he saw as the best for children of all backgrounds and abilities I never had the slightest doubt.

He then seemed to me possibly the most extraordinary man in British public life. He had surfed, without apparently pausing for breath, from the high tide of Thatcherism to the uplands of New Labour. Education Secretaries came and went but, for two decades, Sir Cyril was an adviser to all of them. When there was a new idea for schools, he was the man who made it happen and drove it on. In the 1980s, he launched what became fifteen city technology colleges, the most daring educational initiative of Margaret Thatcher's reign. The city academies and the specialist schools, which by 2006 accounted for 85 per cent of all England's secondary schools, were descendants of the CTCs. I reflected that, if this marriage of Thatcherism and Blairism gave birth to a 'world-class' school system, Sir Cyril could claim to be the midwife. 'He's got more influence than any local education authority,' Estelle Morris, former Labour Education Secretary, told me. 'And he's certainly got the ear of No. 10.'

So how did he do it and what drove him? Sir Cyril is not much inclined to reflection or self-analysis and, without being exactly reticent about himself, he prefers to answer most questions by thrusting tables of statistics at you, supposedly proving the amazing success of academies. But so far as I could discover from what he and others told me, four qualities were crucial: missionary zeal, a belief in traditional values, an appetite for work and an entrepreneur's flair.

The first can be traced to his parents, who were evangelical missionaries, though Sir Cyril said, 'I'm not; I believe in God but I don't go to church.' Born in Yorkshire in 1935, he spent most of his infancy with his mother – his father died before Cyril's birth – in what was then the Belgian Congo. 'Kiluba was all I spoke until I returned to England when I was six,' he explained.

The second quality – traditional values – goes back to his schooling at St Marylebone Grammar in London, where he was taught by Thomas Kingston Derry, a distinguished historian and former headteacher of Mill Hill public school, whom Sir Cyril described as 'probably the greatest influence on my life'. Derry was an empire man, who showed his pupils maps of the world with, it seemed, most of the landmass coloured red.

The hard work came at Harvard Business School, where Sir Cyril went, initially on a scholarship, after taking history at Cambridge. 'I had to do three case studies a day,' he recalled. 'One of the purposes of education, I believe, is to teach work habits – doing your homework, doing things on time.' After Harvard, he joined the marketing department of Procter & Gamble in Cincinnati, where his portfolio included Gleam toothpaste, Prell shampoo and Lilt haircare, the selling of which was probably a cinch compared to convincing Labour backbenchers of the merits of academies. 'I had to work even harder. I had to rewrite my first memos ten or twenty times. Every Friday afternoon, I had to write out my key projects for the following week. I learned to prioritise.' And he concluded, with characteristic finality, 'Prioritising. That's one of the weaknesses of government.'

But Sir Cyril was never, by temperament, a corporation man. The entrepreneur in him was evident at Cambridge when – and this was the 1950s, remember – he chartered a DC-6 to take himself and fellow students to do vacation work in America. Later, when his Harvard scholarship ran out, he and two others got the exclusive right to sell and deliver newspapers on campus. Each made $5,000 in clear profit. 'I was the world's highest-paid newspaper boy.' Here, Sir Cyril's voice rose an octave or so, as it often does, and the sentence ended in whoops of laughter. So it was perhaps inevitable that, before long, he would break away from Procter & Gamble and, with two friends, start his own business.

His wife was an American high school teacher, and she wanted to take a group to France, but found the only organisation that did such trips was full. The result was the American Institute for Foreign Study, which Sir Cyril still runs and which takes him frequently to America, giving him a faintly Mid-Atlantic accent. 'We mailed high school teachers right across the States, and we told them: if they could get eight students, they themselves would get to go free. We had 1,500 students in the first year; now we have 30,000. The three original investors started with an investment of $2,500 each; now the annual turnover's $200m. We're one of the biggest educational enterprises in the world.'

So this, despite its name, is a commercial enterprise? 'We are not aggressively profit-seeking.' But it made him rich? 'It made me a man of independent means.'

Sir Cyril said 'my parents weren't political, they just cared about people', but he himself was clearly a natural Tory. He unsuccessfully fought Huddersfield East and Keighley for the Conservatives in the two 1974 General Elections, and served on the Greater London Council from 1977, when it was Tory-controlled, until 1986, when it wasn't and Thatcher therefore abolished it.

The debate about its abolition first brought him to the attention of Kenneth Baker, then the Environment Secretary. Sir Cyril thought 'the greatest city in the world' should have some form of citywide assembly, and he proposed something not dissimilar to what New Labour eventually adopted more than a decade later. For this heresy, he was denounced by Thatcher at a Downing Street dinner as a wet, a badge he now wears with pride. But it was to him she turned when she wanted someone to organise a conference of industrialists on youth unemployment.

And that was where it all began. 'Margaret spent the whole day there,' recalled Sir Cyril, 'and the employers told her that schools were just not teaching the skills children needed to get jobs.' The solution? The government, bypassing local authority control of schools, should itself set up 100 technology colleges in partnership with business.

Baker was by then Education Secretary and, after he had announced the CTC plans in October 1986, he decided Cyril Taylor was the man to make them happen. 'I needed,' recalled Baker, 'someone who would think laterally and had a roving spirit. I needed someone who would do deals to get us sites. I'm strongly in favour of the Civil Service but the one thing you won't get from it is an entrepreneurial spirit.'

This view – or at least the latter part of it – is one with which Sir Cyril would heartily concur. He lives in a world of whites and blacks – 'don't know' may pass his lips on matters of fact, but not of opinion – and, while all private sponsors of CTCs and city academies are grievously misunderstood, selfless and efficient upholders of the public good, civil servants, along with local education authorities, are among the planet's dark forces. His favourite story is that when he moved in to take charge of the CTC scheme, the education department had already received donations. The civil servants had put the cheques in a box, which they brought to him. 'They didn't know what to do with them you see [whoops of laughter].'

The CTCs had a chequered history, mainly because the building costs were twice what was forecast. Sir Cyril is adamant that 'we could have had a hundred, we had the sponsors lined up', but, after Black Wednesday, the government couldn't afford its share. Instead, he persuaded ministers to switch to converting existing local authority schools and this was the genesis of the specialist schools, the first fifty of which opened in 1994.

Here, Sir Cyril hit on something that, as it turned out, would make his ideas acceptable to Labour. CTCs were exclusive, but specialist schools, offering excellence in particular areas such as science, arts, sports or languages, were inclusive. Any school – or almost any school – could become specialist. The few that weren't good enough, it was eventually decided, would be re-branded as academies, themselves essentially a re-branding of the CTC idea, as reinterpreted by Sir Cyril's close ally, Andrew Adonis, Tony Blair's education adviser and later the schools minister. And so – hey presto! – the nation would be on the road to 'world-class' schools, all under Sir Cyril's energetic guidance.

It was on a train journey to Darlington in December 1996 with Blair, to open a specialist school, that he had converted the then opposition leader to his mission. So Sir Cyril, knighted in 1989 for services to the Thatcherite project, left the Conservative party in 1997 ('I know I'll have to give it up,' he is reported to have said, as though it were some furtive nocturnal habit) and served the Blairite project, for which he was knighted a second time in 2004. (Did this make him Sir Sir Cyril Taylor? Apparently not. He is styled Sir Cyril Taylor, GBE, which stands for Knight Grand Cross of the Most Excellent Order of the British Empire, the second gong being a cut above your plain Knight Bachelor.) He sounds like an opportunist, but nobody who knows him thinks he is.

'It was clear he was just keener on specialist schools than he was on Toryism,' said Estelle Morris. 'He is genuinely committed to the public good,' said Charles Clarke, another former Labour Education Secretary. 'I never detected any self-interest, or even vanity.' Not that anybody found him easy to work with. That messianic conviction and that energy never tolerated much opposition and, if he encountered it, he would be marching off to No. 10. It is a tribute to his charm, ability and sincerity that some former Education Secretaries – and he worked for ten successive holders of this office – were aggrieved by this political sharp practice, but still concluded that, all in all, he was a good egg. After all, Sir Cyril never took a penny in remuneration (or even, he says, expenses) for all this effort.

I met him a second time in 2006 at London's Queen Elizabeth Hall, where the Croydon-based BRIT School for Performing Arts was holding a concert. The school is a hybrid of CTC and specialist school in which Sir Cyril takes particular pride. 'Mrs Thatcher shouted, yes shouted, that she wasn't having a school to produce out-of-work actors but we persuaded her this was a growth area [whoops of laughter].'

As we met for the BRIT School's concert, the first parents' legal challenge to the academy programme was being heard in the courts. Sir Cyril brushed that aside, saying, 'You have to look at the overview; most parents will say an academy is the best thing since sliced bread.' He was similarly dismissive about allegations that a member of his trust council offered peerages for sponsorship cash, cheerfully reporting that more sponsors than ever had come forward since the story broke. There is an engaging innocence about Sir Cyril, who constantly hovers on the brink of indiscretion.

At the concert – which had pop music, videos and modern dance but, to Sir Cyril's regret, lacked 'a piece or two of classical music' – he talked of ability banding and of how schools could form groups over a wide area so that each had its fair share of each band. He also talked of schools in partnership so 'the strong can help the weak; I've talked to lots of heads about it, and they all think it's a terrific idea'. I tried to ask if that included the weak heads, but he was already on to the next idea. 'We need schools to take overall responsibility for vulnerable children. Do you know how many there are?' A flurry of statistics followed. 'That's 6 per cent of all our children who are in care, or at risk of going into care. It's staggering. I'm talking to Alan Johnson [then the Education Secretary] about it.'

Sir Cyril loves to talk new ideas (ideas for doing things, not theories) and sometimes it's hard to keep up. 'He's like a firework you have to point in the right direction,' said a former government adviser.

The following year, Sir Cyril was seized by yet another idea and persuaded me to accompany him to Oldham, scene of bank holiday riots, involving Asians and whites, six years earlier. Subsequent inquiries blamed 'communities leading parallel lives'. Housing was highly segregated and schools, if anything, more so. By 2007, Oldham was in the throes of secondary school reorganisation and, with Sir Cyril's fervent backing, planned to open three multi-faith academies. These would also be 'community schools', serving adults as well as children, on the model pioneered by Henry Morris, chief education officer of Cambridgeshire, more than fifty years previously. Sir Cyril was greatly seized by Morris's vision, which was that 'the duality of education and ordinary life would be abolished'. The application to Oldham was obvious.

I spent an exhausting day with Sir Cyril in Oldham as he toured the city, questioning, cajoling and proselytising. It became evident to me that any attempt to get leaders of different faiths to co-operate – Catholics and Muslims in particular being fiercely protective of their own educational spaces – faced formidable difficulties. But Sir Cyril's enthusiasm and conviction never wavered for a second.

So it always is with him. He is a man of passionate beliefs and hard-headed action and, for better or worse, he has married those attributes in public service more effectively than anybody I know.

Peter Wilby was an education correspondent for the Observer, New Statesman, Sunday Times *and* Independent *before he became an editor. This foreword is an updated and extended version of an article first published in the Guardian on 18 July 2006.*

FOREWORD BY LORD ADONIS

I first met Cyril Taylor shortly after I became Tony Blair's education adviser in the spring of 1998. Cyril was one of the first people to call me – then to write to me, then to send me copies of books he thought might be of interest – all in the space of a few days. He told me he was David Blunkett's adviser on specialist schools – 'as I have been to every Secretary of State since Ken Baker' – and he wanted to brief me in person. 'It ought to be soon because there's a lot going on that you will want to get on top of and it's very important,' he added before I had said anything beyond 'hello'.

I replied, slightly warily, that I would prefer to see a specialist school in action, and perhaps we could talk as we went around? No problem. Within half an hour he was back on the phone with a proposal for us to visit John Kelly School for Girls, a technology specialist school in the North London borough of Brent.

Within a few days we were touring the school. I rapidly appreciated that specialist schools were one of the best things happening in English education and that Cyril Taylor was a remarkable change-maker. John Kelly is located in one of England's most deprived communities. It has since become an academy and exemplifies the transformation in secondary education brought about by school reforms championed by Cyril over the decades.

It is hard to exaggerate Cyril's sheer infectious enthusiasm, and the remarkable combination of passion, information and action he brings to all his activities. It shines through this book. He has personally created and sustained not only movements (notably specialist schools) but also institutions (notably Richmond University and the Specialist Schools and Academies Trust) and causes (notably the needs of gifted and talented students). He has also created one of the most beautiful private gardens in London, and the story of Lexham Gardens, told in Chapter 14, encapsulates all his qualities.

It was a huge privilege to work closely with Cyril on the expansion of specialist schools and later on the creation of academies. Roy Jenkins once told me that the ideal adviser argues to solutions, not to conclusions, and Cyril exemplifies the ideal adviser.

I had always thought of Cyril as a missionary in his zeal. But until reading this book I had not realised that he inherited a genuine missionary gene from his parents. It explains a good deal about him, not least his extraordinary internationalism and his passion to help the poor and underprivileged in practical not rhetorical ways.

Cyril's transatlantic personality is another key theme of this book. It is highly fitting that he is now Chancellor of Richmond, the American International University in London, which owes its foundation, mission and growth very largely to Cyril.

Cyril tells the story of his attempts to enter the House of Commons. He had a lucky escape. He is bigger than party politics, and his influence has been – and continues to be – greater than most holders of ministerial office.

Keynes said it was ideas that rule the world. Churchill said it was institutions. In a sense both were right. It is ideas turned into institutions which shape society, and educational institutions are more powerful in this respect than almost any other. Cyril Taylor has long recognised this, and his influence will endure from this generation to the next and beyond. He is a great man.

Lord Adonis was an architect of education reform under Tony Blair, serving in the No. 10 Policy Unit and then as Minister for Schools from 1998 to 2008. His latest book Education, Education, Education *is published by Biteback books in 2012.*

1

A TODDLER IN AFRICA

My Family & My Early Childhood in the Congo

My parents were both missionaries in Africa. That was how I came to spend my formative years in what was then the Belgian Congo, and is now the troubled nation called the Democratic Republic of the Congo. But by the time that I was born in Leeds on 14 May 1935, my father had died and it was left to my mother, Marjorie, to bring up a family that now included two boys and four girls.

So, I grew up knowing my father through my mother's memories and those of his flock. Father, the Revd Cyril Eustace Taylor, was the son of James Taylor and Clara Annie Podger. James had been born in Pimlico, London in 1856 to Walter and Marion Taylor. My sister Mary has traced our family tree and found that my great-grandfather, Walter, came from Riven Hall in Essex to make his fortune running Taylor's Depository, a furniture store, on Ranelagh Road, Pimlico. It was clearly a successful business, and by the 1881 census, Walter was living with his two sons, James and Albert, with three servants at the Manor House in Teddington, Middlesex, though sadly by this stage he was also a widower.

My grandfather, James, was born in 1856 and worked in the family business for his short life. He died of typhoid fever aged just thirty-nine, in 1895, the same year as his father, Walter. His brother, Albert, took over the business, which he later passed on to his two sons to manage. The Depository would continue to thrive until it was destroyed in the Blitz in September 1940 during the Second World War.[1] My father was just two years old when his father died, having been born in Streatham, in South London, on 24 June 1892. He would be brought up by his mother Clara. Father was educated at Sutton Valance School in Kent and went to read medicine at Trinity Hall in Cambridge when he was twenty years of age.

Father was a remarkable figure, by all accounts. He could have settled for a comfortable life in England as a doctor. But he was within six months of finishing his medical training at Cambridge when he was gripped by the thought of serving God in the Congo. At the age of twenty-eight, he took the boat to Africa in 1920 and became a medical missionary in Ngoimani, in Katanga. My father's inspiration was a remarkable character called James Salter, who had been born into poverty in Preston, Lancashire in 1890. Despite the difficulties of travel during the Great War, Salter managed to get himself to the Congo in 1915, driven largely by a faith in his Pentecostal cause. His followers in the Elim Pentecostal Mission claim that as a result of a constant struggle with malaria, he was raised from his deathbed six times. It was on his return to Britain to recruit more followers that my father heard his message.[2]

My mother, Marjorie Victoria Hebden Taylor, had been bitten by the missionary bug too. She had left another Yorkshire town, Sowerby Bridge near Halifax, in 1922 aged twenty-one, to join the Emmaus Pentecostal Mission – named after the town near Jerusalem where the New Testament says that Jesus appeared to two of his followers after the Resurrection. Emmaus also produced many sterling missionaries.

So it was that two young missionaries from Yorkshire came to meet and marry in Africa. In 1923, after their wedding at Mwanza on 17 October, they moved to the new Ngoimani station. Over the next twelve years, they would have five children, Eustace (Stacey), Patricia, Sylvia, Cynthia and Mary. They toiled together doing what they saw as God's work ceaselessly, establishing a remarkable total of thirty-eight churches with 3,400 believers in fellowship. And during those twelve years, they took just one brief holiday, in South Africa.

Life in Africa was not easy in those days, with a constant presence of disease including malaria. But, it was not in Africa that my father died. The Revd Taylor had returned with Mother on furlough to England, their first trip home since they went to Africa, to pick up his Cambridge Masters' certificate. Before returning to the Congo, he and Mother were on a speaking tour in Switzerland, spreading the missionary message, when he was taken ill with pneumonia. He died in the picturesque town of Vevey on the shores of Lake Geneva, just four months before I was born. He lies in the town cemetery to this day. Just like Father, I was to grow up without a father, and this would make me quite an independent child from an early age.

The Life of the Missionary
It is perhaps difficult these days to imagine the life of a missionary in

the 1930s, but my father was obviously held in great esteem by the people of Ngoimani, so I felt very proud to discover this letter sent by the local people to the Head of the Mission after my father's death in January 1935:

To our Grandmother, Mrs Hester –

All we Christians here in the Church at Ngoi-mani, we have written you this letter with black hearts and tears in our eyes. When we received the telegram sent to Bwana Burton saying that Bwana has died there in the White Man's Land, oh! oh! oh!, don't, don't! the whole Church here had great crying, all the Christians, the old, the young and the teachers, we had terrible crying when we heard of this death. It is true our hearts are very black inside, our Grandmother (Grandmother is a term of great respect) because our hearts were trusting to see the faces of Bwana Taylor and Madame Taylor also. When we received the news of Bwana Taylor's death, yo! yo! yo! our hearts were black. It is our great sorrow because he was our teacher always, to teach us the things of our Lord Jesus Christ, and to cause us to grow in the strong Word of God: because God sent him to this land to see us who were lost in darkness, and to cause us to shine in the things of our Lord. Oh! oh! oh! what can we do? because week by week we always saw Bwana Taylor's letters, because were our hearts not trusting that Bwana would return just now, perhaps in February, perhaps in March. However our hope is lost before our own eyes and before the eyes of all here in Congo, Africa. Oh! oh! oh! Don't! Don't! this death is one which causes every heart here of everybody in the Ngoimani Church of the C. E. M. to be black. Oh! it is our poverty, what shall we do? He was our elder who knew how to shepherd us, he picked us up out of the ditches of suffering and now, what shall we do? We are just dead people because we have lost our teacher here on earth. But up there in heaven we shall see him again before the Lord.

Now we truly sympathise with you in the Name of Jesus Christ, because we had our teacher and all was well here, and who helped us always, but we have poverty now. However we realise that Bwana is now in the hands of the God of Life. We remember many days when we went with him in the work of the Lord, and visited the villages.

But the God of love and peace will put him in a beautiful place. But of course when we see this house in which Bwana Taylor used to live, and all the things that are there, oh! oh! oh! there are only tears in our eyes. But we have God, and He is your God, He who knows how to help you, our Grandmother, and us also.

And now, our Grandmother, we truly sympathise with you, truly our hearts are sore.

How many days was Bwana ill before his death? Because we are truly his friends, we want to know how our teacher died.

We truly sympathise with you Grandmother. We think of your grandchildren – Bwana Eustace, Patsy, Joy, Wendy and Mary – well only God knows how to help them.

Now the church here at Ngoimani want Mrs Taylor saying: 'If the Lord will that Madame Taylor comes to Ngoimani, that will be good.'

We sympathise greatly in the Name of our Lord Jesus Christ. May the God of love and peace be with you always.

But, remarkably, Mother was determined to continue their joint mission in the Congo. Just six months after my birth, she set sail again for Africa. She decided not to bring all six of her children with her this time. Much to their disappointment, my three elder sisters were left with their paternal grandmother in the Sussex seaside town of Worthing, the sedateness of which they saw as no match for the excitement of an African missionary village. My brother went to Fulneck School in Yorkshire, where he lived with his maternal grandmother and uncle.

Marjorie Taylor was then thirty-four years of age and, accompanied by my youngest sister Mary and myself, spent two months at sea travelling to the Congo via Cape Town and up Lake Tanganyika before we put in at Kabumbulu, 15 miles from the mission station. Our welcome was uproarious. Crowds thronged the bank of the Congo River. Much to her embarrassment, my mother was carried aloft amid shouts of joy, songs of praise and torrents of prayer. My mother later wrote that she felt like 'a crumb seized by an army of ants'. However, the affection was genuine and made up in part for the sad loss of my father and the separation from her four older children.

Early Years in the Congo

I stayed with Mother in the missionary house which she and my father had built in the hills above the Congo village. We were living in a very remote area, with no major towns nearby. There were certainly no hospitals or schools. It was an exciting place for a toddler, but it was no place to gain any formal education. Mary, two years older than me, was sent back to be with her sisters in Worthing two years after our return, in 1937, when she was four.

I grew up getting to know many of the local people, and learned their language before I learned English. Kiluba is one of two Bantu languages spoken in that part of Congo to this day. I was taught to read Kiluba by Matthew, my personal attendant, who took care of me when my mother was busy with missionary work. I'm afraid I no longer remember any of the language, though I would later acquire a fluency in Swahili. The only other Europeans in the area were Miss Amy Entwhistle and Miss Emmeline Bartlett, who lived nearby and were also medical missionaries. When I eventually learned to speak English at the age of five, I developed a very bad stammer.

As a small boy, I came to see some extraordinary sights that were denied to my sisters in more tranquil Worthing. I was experiencing nature in the raw, and some events have stayed with me to this day. I have always loved dogs, and one of my saddest memories is when an eagle swooped down from the sky and picked up and killed my little spaniel. During those early years in the Congo, I also developed an aversion to snakes. The country still has over twenty breeds of venomous snake, so it was a fear that was hardly irrational. Some snakes are even eaten, but I preferred to stay well away from them. My fear of snakes also helped me to develop a sixth sense when the reptiles were close by. On one occasion, I noticed that there was a snake in the kitchen where Mother was cooking supper. Shouting loudly, I ensured that she avoided the fatal bite of the black mamba, a 3-metre-long creature with a reputation as one of the most poisonous snakes in the world. It is no exaggeration to say that my sixth sense helped save Mother's life.

Father had been a keen gardener, and I too developed green fingers at the mission station. Mother showed me how to plant a vegetable patch, where I grew my own carrots and spinach. But they were often no match for the wild boar that frequently trampled and ate my proud plants before they were ready for harvesting. Years later, in London, I would turn my keenness for gardening into the transformation of a very different patch of land, in Kensington. But that's for another chapter.

The Journey Home

The outbreak of the Second World War was to bring to an end my four years growing up in Africa. I would return in a different way to this fascinating continent as a young man. But Mother felt that the war meant it was right to return to England, and we embarked on the long but memorable journey home early in 1941. The two of us travelled through the Congo forests and hills, being carried on a sedan chair – with four poles carried by two porters – to our ship on Lake Tanganyika which took us into Northern Rhodesia (now Zambia). We travelled to the Zambezi River, where I first saw the Victoria Falls, one of the great sights of Africa. From Rhodesia we boarded the southern section of the great Cape to Cairo railway to Cape Town. I was just five years of age, but I still remember the excitement of taking that great train, on the railway first envisioned by Cecil Rhodes.

But it was wartime, and ships back to England were irregular. So we had to spend a few months in Cape Town, staying at a local missionary home, before we could start the last leg of our journey home. When we finally boarded a ship, my most vivid memory is that I was given a long clothesline to play with. It kept me occupied for quite a while. I would pretend to be fishing with the rope, until one day, while 'fishing', I dropped the rope overboard. I started to climb over the side of the ship to jump down into the water and retrieve the rope. This was not a great idea in the middle of the Atlantic Ocean. Perhaps it was divine intervention or maybe my five-year-old self was seized with a sudden rush of good sense, but I thought better of it. That I lived to tell the tale shows what a lucky escape I had.

Of course, a wandering clothesline was not the only hazard facing us as we sailed up the African coast towards war-torn Europe. The Atlantic was a hotbed of German U-boats and warships. The ship's alarms went off several times during the two months we were at sea, indicating the presence of a German warship. Fortunately, no attack took place on our ship, although a neighbouring ship was attacked by a torpedo and it tragically did sink.

Even on the approach to Liverpool – or perhaps especially so – we were not safe. Just before we landed ourselves, I remember seeing a ship sinking in the Irish Sea. It had been torpedoed. To say it was a great relief to land safely in Merseyside is an understatement.

But it was also quite a shock for me to return to England. I was just five years of age. Aside from the journey home, all I had known was a Congolese mission station. I barely spoke any English, and I had a very bad stammer. But we had arrived safely, and the next phase of my childhood could begin.

2

A PERIPATETIC CHILDHOOD

Growing up in Yorkshire & London &
My Proposals for Children in Care

Not unlike many wartime children, I found myself living away from my mother in the first year back in England. But I was not being sent to the country to avoid the ravages of the Blitz. Mother wanted to raise money for the Congo mission station, so she embarked on a speaking tour of Elim churches. Stacey stayed in Yorkshire and my sisters in Worthing, where they were at the Mount School.

That was why I came to spend a year living with a caring but childless couple called the Ramsbottoms in the Yorkshire town of Knottingley, near Wakefield. In one sense the Ramsbottoms were like many foster parents today, and Mother was paying them to care for me. Away from the snakes and wild boar of the Congo mission station, I found companionship in a less aggressive creature in Knottingley. I grew very fond of their cocker spaniel called Rough, and spent many a happy hour playing with him. I also had a chance to exercise my green fingers again, as growing vegetables was a wartime necessity, and had as much a place in the Knottingley garden as in allotments across Britain. I also learnt how to use an air rifle.

But this was also a strange time for a young boy of six. I was in a new country, living with strangers. I had to learn English rapidly. At the local primary school, I was placed with children who were a year younger than me, because the teachers felt I needed to catch up with the rest of the school. As a result, I was bullied and teased quite badly by the other children. I'm sure that is what brought on my stammer, something that would stay with me for much of my life.

Overcoming a stammer is all about confidence, and I was struck by the techniques shown in the film *The King's Speech* in 2010 when the Australian speech therapist Lionel Logue is depicted giving King George VI the confidence to make public speeches. I spent much of the first two decades of my life with a stammer, but I also discovered how important confidence was in overcoming it. I remember going on the London Tube one day and seeing a big poster asking, 'Do you stammer? I can help you.' I went to the man behind the advertisement – unfortunately, I can no longer remember his name – and he would send me out on little expeditions such as going to the Grosvenor Hotel to check a bag in. He told me that my problem was basically one of confidence. That's where the improvement started, and it was helped further by going into the Army and becoming an officer. But it never completely disappeared until I came back to Britain from the United States and had to make political speeches.

An Interest in Children in Care

Despite the teasing and bullying, I had some happy times in my year away from Mother. But I also missed her, and the experience would give me a lifelong personal interest in how we look after children in care, particularly those who are fostered or in children's homes, and a great empathy for those who are looked after by others. I have tried not only to influence policy, but also to help individuals, where and when I can.

I would start to take an interest in the issue as High Sheriff of Greater London in the mid-1990s, when I focused on young offenders and visited the Feltham Young Offenders Institution several times. Around that time too, I visited Centrepoint, the remarkable charity for homeless young people, and was told that if I found young people living on the street I could put them in a taxi and send them to their shelter, giving my name. I still do that to this day. But my own fostering experience encouraged me to look more closely at the wider picture and potential solutions.

The fact is that the 65,000 children in care in Britain and the 320,000 in need of care get the rawest of deals from our education and social services system. A quarter of young offenders at Feltham had been in care. Of those permanently looked-after children in England at any one time,[3] 48,310 of these children are placed with foster carers, 7,910 are living in children's homes and other residential accommodation, with a further 2,450 placed for adoption. The Fostering Network estimates there is a shortage of at least 8,000 good foster families. Where they are successful in finding families, the total annual cost of a child in foster care is close to £20,000, with some independent fostering agencies charging up to £50,000 per child. The foster carer, however, typically only receives £200 per week. The average annual cost of residential care in special children's homes is much higher, at £114,000 per child, in some cases £200,000. The total annual direct cost of looking after the 60,000 children in care is £2.4 billion, or £40,000 per child.

Despite this huge investment of resources, the outcomes are distressingly inadequate. Children in care perform poorly in tests and exams. Only 43 per cent of eleven-year-olds reach expected standards in English and Maths, compared with 74 per cent of all children, and just 13 per cent of children in care for a year or more obtain five good GCSE grades compared to 58 per cent for all children. The attainment gap has been growing in recent years.[4] This then means that many don't stay in education or full-time training: only 74 per cent of looked-after children are still in full-time learning after sixteen compared with 92 per cent of other young people. Moreover, between a quarter and a third of people sleeping rough were in care.

Nine per cent of looked-after children aged ten or over are cautioned or convicted for an offence each year – three times the rate for all young people of this age. Sadly, many of those cautioned will become serial offenders who will be in and out of prison most of their lives. Indeed, one study showed that a quarter of all adults in prison had been in care for at least part of their childhood.[5]

This is pretty dismal data. Not only is it costing the taxpayer large sums of money to care for children who are unable to live with their parents but the outcomes are simply unacceptable. Moreover the real cost of failing to look after our vulnerable children is much greater than the £2.4 billion of direct costs. A study published by the London School of Economics showed that the overall costs in any one year are close to £10 billion if 'knock on' costs are added, including the costs of young offenders, welfare bills and higher-than-average health needs.

Children in care frequently change both their home and their school. As many as one in eight children in care experience three or more placements a year, with serious negative effects in terms of their emotional and behavioural difficulties. How can any child flourish in such circumstances?

Effective action at an early stage could prevent these children having to be taken into care at a later stage. Having looked into the issue and talked to many in the field, I developed policy proposals which I still believe would be of value today.

One of the most radical would be to arrange for children in care to be looked after jointly by local authority children's services and the schools which they attend. A key to improving provision for vulnerable children must be to provide greater stability. Local authority children's services and schools are now supposed to ensure that schools and children's services work more closely together. Improvements are also being made in the adoption procedures but much more needs to be done. Local networks of good schools could also provide support, but a more radical solution is required.

Peter Crook, when he was principal of the Harris Peckham Academy in South London, used to argue that care for looked-after children could be improved if schools were more closely involved. This could include, on a voluntary basis, responsibility for helping to find and for supervising foster parents. Legal responsibility for the assignment of care status to children would still remain with the local authority. More of the day-to-day responsibility could be performed by the school, perhaps through the provision of social services staff in schools. This would include the counselling of pupils and liaising with foster parents.

Peter told me that he had about fifteen looked-after children and a further 100 children in need of care attending his academy. Once he noticed that one of these children was absent from school. When he contacted the foster family he was told the child had been moved to another family but he could not be told who or where they were. If the school received even a proportion of the funds currently spent on looked-after children, he believed that they could employ the social workers themselves and have trained counsellors, necessary to do a better job of keeping the education as well as the welfare of looked-after children on track. Of course, heads would work with social services rather than trying to replace them.

The Sydney Russell School in Barking persuaded the local authority to delegate supervision of the school's twelve children in care to one of its teachers, Anne-Marie McNamara. She supervises both the children in care and their foster parents. The results are impressive, with much better academic results and fewer changes in foster parents.

When I presented my ideas to the Labour MP Alan Johnson, when he was Education Secretary, he spoke from personal experience when he told me that we must not write off such children as unfit for the world of education. 'It is our responsibility to make the education system fit the needs of all children,' he said. 'If we are to raise every child's educational attainment, we need to take a more personalised approach to teaching for each and every child.' Alan had himself been in care and has argued passionately that we must improve the care given to vulnerable children.

If responsibility for pupils was given to schools on a joint basis with social services, local networks of schools could collaborate to employ specialist counsellors. Alternatively, particular foster parents could receive specialist counsellor training and act as supervisors for other foster parents and receive additional payment. Some schools now use minibuses to bring children in care to school and this can help to avoid such children having to change schools when they change foster parents. A substantial number of looked-after children, especially those with emotional, behavioural and social difficulties, are enrolled in special schools including some special boarding schools run by organisations such as the Priory Group. Where this is the right solution for them, more children in care should be placed in special schools.

I would then assign a mentor to every child in care. Many looked-after children do not develop an effective relationship with the social services person assigned to look after them. The reasons are manifold including the turnover of social services staff and the large number of looked-after children – as many as thirty assigned to a particular social services official. A particular problem is that in some local authorities, social services assign responsibility for looked-after children on a group 'territorial' basis, rather than giving responsibility for a particular child to a specific social worker.

Charles Parker, clerk of the Mercers' Company in 2006, told me that many of the 24,000 City of London liverymen and women would be willing to act as volunteer mentors for a particular looked-after child. His wife Victoria, a magistrate in Winchester, said that many of the 30,000 magistrates of the courts would also be willing to serve in this role. Mentors would need training as well as screening, and an acceptable framework would be needed to allow regular contact and meetings, liaison with schools and discussion with social services.

But there should be minimal bureaucratic procedures. The relationship between mentors and their assigned child should be primarily routed through the headteacher of the child's school.

Foster parents would welcome better training. Most foster families are dedicated and caring. They simply wish to provide the very best possible care for the children assigned to them. Many looked-after children, however, have behavioural difficulties which require specialist expertise and considerable dedication. It is therefore important foster parents have the skills to support them properly. Other sources of providing foster parents such as religious groups should also be sought. Data is important too, and while the government does now publish more data than before on looked-after children, there is room for more detail, at least in a readily accessible format.

Another key issue is the unacceptable bureaucratic procedure used to approve the adoption of children in care by families looking to adopt a child. The current procedure for adoption can last up to thirty months. The government has recently announced that subject to certain safeguards, a family wishing to adopt a particular child in care will be engaged as foster parents for that child while their application to adopt the child is being processed. Successive governments have made such commitments, yet the number of adoptions has fallen in recent years.

Boarding Places

Perhaps my most radical suggestion to Alan Johnson – and one that I still believe has considerable merit – is that children in care should be placed where possible in boarding schools. While boarding schools would only be able to accept a small proportion of the total, even a 5 per cent target – or 3,000 places a year – would be a great step forward. We currently have thirty-six state boarding schools with some 4,000 boarders with the average boarding charge being around £7,000 per year, and some academies are developing new boarding provision. Their fees are much less than the cost of a foster family placement, and dramatically less than the cost of residential care, although additional arrangements would need to be made for school holidays.

Charities, such as the Royal National Children's Foundation, arrange for hundreds of vulnerable children to attend independent boarding schools each year. The Royal Alexandra and Albert School, a state boarding school in Reigate, has some fifty children in care. They do exceptionally well and get on well with their fellow students. It costs about £25,000 per bedroom to build a dormitory, or £2.5 million for 100 beds. Even with the annual recurrent boarding costs of £7,000 per year per child, the cost of boarding school provision would be dramatically less than it costs a council to run a children's home. There would be much better outcomes, not least in exam results, if we made the change.

The record of independent boarding schools such as Christ's Hospital and state-maintained boarding schools such as the Royal Alexandra & Albert School in Reigate in looking after children in care is excellent. If the political will is there, it should not be so difficult to find 3,000 boarding school places. Additional boarding places could be provided in a number of ways. State boarding schools should expand – as has already happened at Wymondham College in Norfolk. If all the state boarding schools agreed to expand their provision of beds by just 100 places and agreed to reserve 20 per cent of their total provision (including existing beds) for looked-after children we would have nearly 1,500 boarding places available. I have estimated the annual cost of such provision, allowing for the repayment of any private sector loans, to be £15,250,000. This is just £10,517 per child, much less than the cost of fostering or a placement in a children's home. The taxpayer would save £7.5 million a year. Of course, all this would require the consent of the school, the child and the family or guardian.

Clearly, those with severe behavioural problems could not be placed in a regular boarding school since they would disrupt the education of the other pupils. Such children belong in residential special schools such as the Priory special needs boarding school. 1,100 looked-after children are already placed in residential special schools, some all year round.

Academies have an important role to play too. Some like Durand Academy in South London are even planning their own boarding secondary school. Others should consider adding a boarding unit of fifty beds or so, as The Harefield Academy in Uxbridge, Middlesex has done since 2011. If enough other academies followed suit, we might have 7,500 more places for children in care.

Assuming that just 20 per cent of boarding places should be for looked after children to ensure a balanced intake, adding boarding units in fifty day schools could make 1,000 places available for looked-after children with savings to the taxpayer of £5 million but would require a demand for the balance of 4,000 places from parents willing to pay the £7,000 per child annual fee. It would also provide more affordable boarding places for other families whose jobs – including in the military – might make such an option necessary.

Finally, and perhaps most importantly, we should accept the generous offer of independent boarding schools, both primary and secondary, to accept a number of children in care. The 600 independent boarding schools, of which 200 are secondary and 400 are preparatory schools, have agreed in principle to accept five children each for a total of 3,000 places. The Boarding Schools' Association has indicated that for a fee of £12,000 per child (a tuition allowance similar to state day schools of £5,000 plus the average cost of boarding in a state boarding school of £7,000) many of their member schools would be willing to take up to five looked-after children each. This would save the taxpayer £39 million a year compared with the cost of providing accommodation in a foster family while attending a local school. By agreeing to do this the independent schools would not only be doing good, but could also safeguard their charitable status as well as widening the diversity of their student intake.

The trauma of abuse and neglect experienced by many looked-after children prior to entering care must, of course, be acknowledged. These children need emotional support to overcome their previous abuse and mistreatment. Boarding schools taking in looked-after children would need specialist staff trained to care for these children. A charter of rights for children in care would ensure that their interests were protected with the right to an adult monitoring and better monitoring of their care provision. For an improvement in the care given to looked-after children, we will need to achieve fundamental changes in attitude in the way local authorities handle vulnerable children. Their educational welfare and not just their physical welfare must be made the priority. I will certainly continue to press for better integration between educational and social care services.

We must address legislative regulations about the problems of looked-after children as well as reviewing adoption procedures. We should also remove bureaucratic barriers which prevent use of boarding schools for vulnerable children. If local authorities' confidence in the greater use of boarding schools is to be achieved, the boarding school sector must demonstrate how they can engage with the families, carers and communities of the children placed in order to minimise the potential negative impact of separation of vulnerable children from their families and of distance from home. They must also train their teachers even more than they do already in the skills necessary to look after vulnerable children. Many boarding schools already have very high standards of care for looked-after children. But we need to increase the number of boarding schools with carers trained to look after vulnerable children.

Put simply, my own experience taught me that we need to have a fundamental rethink of our approach to the problem. I have seen how many headteachers find themselves acting as surrogate parents for children in care, and there is room to formalise this role by giving them joint responsibility with social services for these young people. That could help transform the frankly abysmal GCSE results that would give these children the leg up they need in life. For some, boarding school is an attractive – and much less costly – alternative. As Tony Blair, whom I would come to know and respect as Prime Minister, put it when he was launching one of his social exclusion reports, 'If we are serious about building a prosperous, fair and strong society then every child, whatever their background, must have the chance to make the most of their talents and potential. That is true for a child in care as much as for any other child.'

It is rare in government that there is the opportunity simultaneously to do good and to save the taxpayer substantial funds. I hope that all parties will find ways to ensure that children in care get the start in life they so richly deserve. My own experience of a sort of foster care would come to an end in 1942, when the Taylor family was finally reunited.

Scarborough Years

In that year, we all moved to the seaside town of Scarborough, a popular and beautiful resort on the East Coast of Yorkshire. Shortly after our reunification, we settled at Dearne Villa, a house in Scalby on the outskirts of the town. I was seven, but this was the first time I had seen most of my siblings. My sisters, in particular, deeply resented that they had been left in Worthing under the care of their grandmother and had seen so little of Mother. There were only three bedrooms so we had to share. However, though the house was small, it was also detached and we had access to allotments next door.

As a seven-year-old, I was starting to feel the ill effects of my time in the Congo. I suffered attacks of malaria that were alarming at the time, though I did recover from them and have had no recurrences. Nevertheless, I was particularly pleased to be reunited with Mary, who was closest to me in age of all my siblings. I'm afraid we got up to a lot of mischief together, and had occasional fights, but we were usually quickly put right by Mother. On occasions, Mary and I used to go to a local stationery shop where we sometimes stole pencils. When Mother found out about this, she made us return them to the shop and apologise to the stationer. Embarrassed by having to say sorry so publicly, we learnt in a very practical way the difference between right and wrong.

But Scarborough felt like a real breath of fresh air, with its rural surroundings and fishermen landing their catches in the harbour. We all had bicycles, and I used to go cycling into the woods with Mary for picnics. I had plenty of friends there too. Yet, this was still wartime, and we had a soldier billeted with us who lived in our garage, though he kept himself to himself, and organised his own meals.

We had to take our turn doing chores. Mother would give each of us a list of jobs to do each day, including cleaning and washing up. This taught us all to live together as a family doing our specific duties. But I was particularly pleased that my love for gardening could be kept up, as we all had our own piece of land to grow vegetables on the allotments adjoining our house. I grew potatoes and was so anxious to see how they were doing that I was constantly digging them up. Of course, that hardly helped their growth. This time, I couldn't blame the wild boars for messing things up.

When we moved to Scarborough, I first went to the local primary school which was part of Scarborough Boys' High School, which Stacey also attended. The school was very strict, and I still remember getting the cane for my occasional misbehaviour, but the lessons there did ignite a love of history that has stayed with me to this day. Stacey was accepted by Trinity Hall, Cambridge, where our father had studied, but he first had to join the Navy where he saw active service on a destroyer patrolling the Arctic Ocean in 1944 and 1945. He would later become an Anglican priest, working mainly in Canada and the United States. Stacey passed away in 2002.

Halifax Days

We didn't stay long in Scarborough. Within two years, we moved some 80 miles inland to Halifax, a lot closer to the Leeds of my birth. I was certainly seeing a lot of Yorkshire in my youth. My grandmother – on my mother's side – Margaret Hebden and my uncle, William Hebden, lived in Sowerby Bridge, on the outskirts of Halifax. It was in this Calder Valley market town that I was to see the end of the war in May 1945. By now a growing ten-year-old, I celebrated by parading up and down a hill near our new home waving the Union Jack as furiously and patriotically as any of the delighted local population.

We spent a year at Kebroyd House with our in-laws, and it was there that I learnt the skill of carpentry. My uncle, who had inherited a healthcare business from his father which included the manufacture of shampoos, arranged for me to spend Saturday mornings working with a local carpenter. William Hebden was also a keen genealogist – long before the days of *Who Do You Think You Are?* he traced the Hebden family back 1,000 years to the Dukes of Northumberland, a lineage that included the legendary Sir Henry Percy, or Harry Hotspur, the thirteenth-century warrior whose rebellion against King Henry IV would lead to his own untimely end. Working with Procter & Gamble in my later life, I clearly took more from my uncle's side than from my livelier antecedents.

A year after arriving in Sowerby Bridge, Mother purchased Whinneyfields, a house in Huddersfield Road closer to the centre of Halifax. My uncle William moved in with us. When we came to Sowerby Bridge, I had been sent to the local primary school, but once we moved nearer the centre of town, I was lucky enough to be sent to Halifax New School, a small private school, where an inspirational teacher finally taught me to read well. This was a time when I was particularly happy at school, and I also developed my love of sports there, playing hockey every day. It was while at Halifax New School that I passed my Eleven plus and gained a place at Heath Grammar School, a famous old Halifax school.

Alas, this good fortune only lasted for a term. We were soon on the move again. My mother, for reasons which I never fully discovered, suddenly decided to move to Leeds where she bought a house close to Armley Jail. I was admitted to Roundhay Grammar School in Oakwood, where I spent the next year. Even that involved yet another home move, to a house in Lady Edith's Drive, so that I could be closer to my school. Forty years later, I persuaded Sir Evelyn de Rothschild to donate substantial funds to Roundhay School to enable it to become one of the first specialist Technology Colleges.

This was also the time when my older sisters, Pat, Sylvia and Cynthia, all left home to start their careers. Pat, who was born in 1927, became the first lady photographer for the *Yorkshire Post*. One of her most famous shots was a picture of Prince Charles as a child. I still enjoy staying with her and her husband Douglas Inch in their Yorkshire home. Sylvia, two years younger than Pat, trained as a horticulturist in Kent and later became a freelance stylist working for advertising film producers and photographers, before becoming a landscape gardener. Having retired to Devon, she sadly passed away in 2012. Cynthia – whom we called Wendy – was born in 1930 and became a nurse. She also passed away in 2012.

By the time my sisters left, Mary and I were bickering a lot, possibly because she thought Mother favoured me. But these were the inevitable tensions of young siblings, and we get on very well these days. Having enjoyed a career as an occupational therapist on both sides of the Atlantic, she has retired to Devon, where I sometimes stay with her and her husband Daniel. She received an MBE for her services to the elderly in 2000.

A Move to the Capital

My Yorkshire days were over by 1947. Six years after returning from Africa, I would find myself starting life as a teenager in London. Mother's inherited money had run out and she needed to find a job to support those of us who were still at home. She found a position as the assistant matron of the Church of England girls' hostel in Baker Street where I lived in a small room previously used as a storage area. It had windows both looking outside and inside, so sometimes the girls would look in on me.

I was accepted by the nearby St Marylebone Grammar School where I could settle into my studies for the next seven years. St Marylebone was originally the Philological School founded by Thomas Collingwood, under the patronage of Prince Frederick, the son of King George III, in 1792. Its first buildings were in what is now Stanhope Street, and it moved to the Marylebone Road in 1827. Among its distinguished alumni are the authors Jerome K. Jerome and Len Deighton, and the historian Eric Hobsbawm.

For much of the twentieth century, it was under the aegis of the London County Council, though it was to be closed in 1981 by the Inner London Education Authority, as a result of the drive for comprehensive education. Attempts to merge it with the nearby secondary modern school had failed.

When I arrived in those post-war years, St Marylebone was a thriving grammar school with a mixed group of boys. The school would give me stability in my schooling that had been lacking in my moves around Yorkshire, and my studies progressed well. I gained a particular love for languages – though I had few opportunities to practice my Kiluba – and history. The school was very competitive, and not just at sports. A fortnightly order was published, ranking each boy in each form according to the marks obtained in the tests and work submitted. Such extreme accountability certainly worked for me. Soon I was top of my form. During the time I was at St Marylebone from 1947 to 1954 a major influence on my life was Dr Thomas Kingston Derry, a distinguished historian and former headmaster of Mill Hill School. Dr Derry effectively became my surrogate father, taking a personal interest in my welfare and encouraging me to study hard.

It was at St Marylebone that I developed a love of cricket and rugby and also became a runner – the 800 yards was my speciality. I was particularly proud to come second in the London Schools Athletics Days at White City in 1953. But I loved to watch as well as to play, and the highlight was watching Middlesex play cricket. My heroes were Bill Edrich and Denis Compton, both of whom were in their heyday in the late forties. I also gained a love for football in those years, and began my lifelong support for Arsenal. Leslie Compton, at centre half, was a particular favourite. Denis and Leslie were brothers, and both played cricket and football, a rare combination these days. As a boy, I would watch the game from the terraces at the old Arsenal stadium. More recently, thanks to my good friend Lord Harris of Peckham, who is a director of the club, I have enjoyed match tickets to watch from the Directors' Box at the new Emirates Stadium.

Mother Moves Again, But I Stay Put

At St Marylebone I was doing well and enjoying the experience enormously. So while Mother's work meant that she needed to move again, I was grateful to be able to stay at the same school. Mother became the matron of Elim Woodlands, a Pentecostal Missionary Home in Clapham, south of the River Thames in 1950. This meant a long cycle to school that caused me to start being late, a potentially serious threat to my career. So, when Mother moved back to Yorkshire a year later to become matron of a missionary house in Ilkley, I insisted on staying in the capital. I was sixteen at the time, and studying for the School Certificate, an examination that was soon to be replaced by O-levels.

This was a key decision in my life. I was strongly supported in making it by Dr Derry, by then a huge influence on me. Arrangements were made for me to stay at the Methodist International House (MIH) on Inverness Terrace in Bayswater, which was both close to my school and a hostel for young people from all over the world. The matron, Mrs Sharpus, used to say that the initials MIH reversed spelt Him, giving it an extra spiritual dimension. Staying at MIH meant I no longer had to miss classes as it was but a short Tube ride to school. I could also throw myself more into the life of the school, becoming a prefect and Abbot House Captain. I entered wholly into the spirit of the system by helping Abbot win Best House in 1953.

I benefited too from the international nature of the hostel. I shared a room with a very helpful student from Ceylon (now Sri Lanka) called Claude Fonseka, who was working for the HSBC bank. Without his help in Maths revision I might never have got to Cambridge. Even with his help, I had to take the exam three times before securing a pass. I was luckier with my other School Certificate exams, securing passes (there were no grades then, just pass or fail) in Latin, Greek, French and Italian, as well as English, English Literature, History, Geography and (eventually) Maths. My wife, Judy, and I were delighted to be able to meet Claude many years later in Colombo when we were visiting the area on a cruise. I had the chance to thank him again for the help he gave me with that crucial maths exam.

Mother only stayed a year in Yorkshire before returning to the capital in 1952 to become matron of the Church of England missionary home on Finchley Road. I moved back in with her again, saying goodbye to the Bayswater hostel. This was also the time when I took my A-level exams in History, French and Latin. But Mother soon moved again to another job, first in Southampton and later in Westminster. I decided that it would be easier for my studies to make the YMCA off Tottenham Court Road my base while studying for my Trinity Hall Cambridge scholarship examination which I took in December 1953. I shared a room this time with a Burmese student. Thanks to all that encouragement from Dr Derry and my teachers at St Marylebone, the nervous boy who had arrived from Africa barely speaking English won a place at Cambridge and a London County Council scholarship which paid for all my fees including board and lodging.

Those first eighteen years of my life taught me several lessons. I had lived in twelve different homes and towns. My peripatetic childhood taught me to value stability in my own life greatly. At the MIH hostel, as well as learning how to play ping pong and snooker from the other residents, all of whom were university-age students, being a sixteen-year-old among so many young people in their twenties helped me to grow up faster than I would have otherwise. It was also a challenge living as a young teenager with university-aged students who were several years older than me. I fell in love with a beautiful but older Anglo-Indian girl from Madras. Unfortunately, she did not return my affections. It was during these years, because of meagre financial resources, that I also learned to live frugally. Of course, frugality was common with wartime rationing lasting into early 1950s, but being brought up by a hard-working single mother made it harder than for other classmates. Those disciplines would serve me well in the Army.

3

GIFTED & TALENTED

Ideas to Enable Highly Able Children to Achieve Their Potential

I gained hugely from my time at St Marylebone, and until the late seventies it was one of many grammar schools open to pupils of all classes. However, those who were not fortunate to pass the Eleven plus found themselves usually in inferior secondary modern schools, and the move to comprehensive education enjoyed support not least from middle-class parents of children who lost out. Education Secretaries including Tony Crosland, Margaret Thatcher and Shirley Williams merged the grammars into new comprehensives. The grammar school closures only ended when Mrs Thatcher became Prime Minister in the early 1980s.

There were good reasons for the move to all-ability comprehensive schools. But one of the unintended outcomes was an assumption that all children should be taught in mixed-ability classes. The view that one size fits all became prevalent. The idea that gifted and talented children should receive special nurturing became anathema to many, who felt it would confer special privileges on a minority of pupils. I profoundly disagree with this view, as I know how important the wonderful education I received at St Marylebone was in getting me a place at Cambridge. My mother could never have afforded a private education for me.

But there are only 164 remaining grammar schools, of which only 2 per cent of their students are eligible for free school meals compared to 16 per cent for all secondary school students, and with the majority of children doing A-levels in comprehensive schools or sixth-form colleges, it is vital that the most able have the chance they deserve to get to the leading universities, as I did. Around one in ten A-level students gains the three A grades that are essential to gain a place at most Russell Group universities, but more than half of them are at independent schools or the remaining grammar schools, even though they account for only a fifth of the candidates. In fact, barely one in twenty A-level candidates at comprehensive schools gains those three A grades, compared with a fifth of those in grammar or independent schools.

Gifted and Talented Provision

These figures suggest that many able children attending comprehensive schools are not realising their potential. Professor David Jesson of York University has shown how less than one third of the 30,000 children who scored in the top 5 per cent in tests at eleven achieved three A-level A grades seven years later at age eighteen. These figures suggest a shocking waste of talent.

The Blair government, through its programme called Excellence in Cities, tried to improve provision for the most able children within comprehensive schools. I was very much involved in helping develop these gifted and talented programmes, which both provided extra classes to stretch pupils within their schools and a national centre based at Warwick University.

The Warwick initiative had its origins in a similar scheme at Johns Hopkins University in the United States, and its President William Brody persuaded Tony Blair, then the Prime Minister, in 2001 that a national institute should be established in England along similar lines to that at his university. Together with Andrew Adonis, Blair's education adviser, I worked with leading educators including Dr Geoff Parks, Director of Admissions at Cambridge University, Stephen Schwartz, Vice Chancellor of Brunel University and Anthony McClaran, Director of the university admissions service UCAS, to establish the National Association for Gifted and Talented Youth (NAGTY) at Warwick. NAGTY spent most of its £5 million budget organising residential summer schools for some 4,000 very able children on the campuses of leading British universities.

By 2007, when NAGTY lost the government contract to manage the gifted and talented programme, it had 150,000 very able children registered as members. NAGTY supported both schools and very able students, as well as serving as a national research centre for gifted and talented education.

I have long believed that data is hugely important in addressing issues. So, I was delighted when Lord Adonis, as schools minister, arranged for the Department for Education and Skills to organise, with the help of Professor Jesson, a national talent search for pupils aged eleven to seventeen in summer 2006. This study identified 30,000 very able eleven-year-old children in each of the last six year groups starting in 1999 – using raw scores in Key Stage 2 tests, given at age eleven, in Maths and English to identify the top 5 per cent of the most able eleven-year-olds in each age cohort. A total of 180,000 names of very able youngsters aged eleven to seventeen were added to a national talent list. Schools were encouraged to add, if they so wished, additional children with talents in other subjects such as music and sport, or late developers. This latter group have been shown to provide substantial additional numbers of those gaining three A grades at A-levels in 2006. All the 3,200 English secondary schools were sent a list of the very able children in their school and asked to give each one of these children the support necessary to realise their potential, including registering them with NAGTY. So far as I know, this was the only national talent search in existence throughout the world, and the government, especially Lord Adonis, was to be commended on this initiative.

By 2007 there was therefore in England, uniquely, both a national talent search and an organisation, NAGTY, in place to support these very able children. However, NAGTY and Warwick lost the contract to manage the gifted children programme in 2007, and the provision organised by the successor organisation, the Centre for British Teaching (CfBT), did not live up to its promise. The problem was that in 2007, an overly complicated tendering document, following European Union guidelines, invited organisations to bid for the right to organise the supply, but not to provide gifted and talented programmes themselves. Warwick decided not to bid for the contract, since they believed they would be unable to ensure its high quality. NAGTY director Deborah Eyre was not even offered a position by the successful bidder, CfBT. This meant that the five years' experience at NAGTY was lost, as the organisation was shut down and its unique expertise was wasted.

CfBT introduced a totally new system. Instead of identifying the children achieving the top 5 per cent test scores in Key Stage 2, all primary and secondary schools were invited to classify 10 per cent of their own children, whatever their ability, as gifted and talented. This meant that some 60,000 children in each age group (there are around 600,000 English children in maintained schools in each age group) were classified as gifted and talented – a total pool of over 700,000 young people aged between five and seventeen. Yet the budget remained at only £5 million, equivalent to only £7 per child per year. Even worse, there were no clear accountability measures to measure the success of the programme. This was an unworkable system and it was no surprise when it was subsequently closed down by Ed Balls when he became Secretary of State in 2007. It has not been revived by the coalition government yet.

Sadly the experience of NAGTY was lost and there is now too little provision for highly able children in too many schools. Schools still receive the names of those children in the top 5 per cent of national ability, and the league tables identify the performance of those who rate in the top third of students nationally. But this is hardly enough to compete in a global economy.

This is why I have argued that we need a new gifted and talented programme. It should use objective criteria to identify the 30,000 children in the top 5 per cent in Maths and English at age eleven. To ensure that it is focused, it should concentrate on secondary age children.

Setting by subject ability should be provided for the most able, with children who show talent at a later age in specific subjects such as maths, science, music or sport included as their performance merits it. A big problem with these programmes is that a significant minority of schools regard them as elitist, so I would classify such education as being as important as other forms of special education, with provision to match. But this programme does need sensible funding, and not the notional £5 million that schools currently have in their general budgets. At a time of austerity it is hard to argue for extra funding, but the cost of a serious £100 million programme – £500 for each gifted and talented child – would be greatly outweighed by the economic benefits. Additional funding might be raised from charities and other sources.

This framework is essential for the creation of an effective gifted and talented programme. In addition to the recommendation that the new academies offer both technical and academic streams at age fourteen, including gifted and talented provision, other measures could be used.

Saturday morning classes could be organised with a nearby university, or if there is not one close by, a high-performing school or a private school. The record of programmes such as the Royal College of Music Junior Department has been outstanding in nurturing talent – a substantial proportion of the Royal College's undergraduate intake comes from its Saturday Junior Department courses. Dr Martin Stephens, the former headteacher of St Paul's Boys' School, provided a gifted maths programme on Saturday mornings for twenty pupils from nearby specialist comprehensive schools in Hammersmith, with support from the government. It should be possible to provide two hours of Saturday morning classes for forty weeks for £200 per child per year. Weekly Saturday morning classes should be given equal priority to summer schools.

Both non-residential and residential summer courses could be provided at leading universities and private schools, with part of the cost being borne by the secondary schools, by parents where they can afford to pay, or by sponsored scholarships. These courses would have clear and demanding syllabuses.

The Summer Institute for the Gifted

Through the American Institute for Foreign Study, I have tried to foster extra support for gifted children in the United States. The Summer Institute for the Gifted (SIG), which has been organised for AIFS by the National Society for the Gifted and Talented since 1985, runs a very successful programme for some 3,000 gifted and talented US and foreign children. These programmes last three weeks and accept students aged nine to seventeen. Classes are hosted at ten of the leading universities in the US, including Princeton, Berkeley and Yale.

About a quarter of SIG students are on scholarships with another quarter coming from outside the US. The criteria used to select students are similar to those which we used in the English national talent search – they are within the top 5 per cent of the ability range. I have always enjoyed meeting students at the SIG campuses, where in addition to the residential summer schools, day-long programmes and Saturday morning classes are offered throughout the year.

A typical SIG curriculum includes a selection of courses from the humanities, maths, science and technology, multi-disciplinary subjects and visual and performing arts (see Appendix 2).

A particular problem for gifted and talented children from socially disadvantaged areas is that they are often regarded as 'weirdos' or 'nerds' by their peer group. It is not cool to be a hard-working gifted and talented child in many schools, especially those in socially disadvantaged areas. Enrolment with 200 similarly gifted and talented children of the same age in a summer school at a prestigious university such as Princeton can change a child's life because they are surrounded by able peers. I vividly remember chatting to a very bright young African-American girl from Harlem attending the SIG campus at Princeton on a full scholarship. I asked if she liked the programme. She said she loved it. When asked why, she replied, 'I don't have to pretend to be dumb here to make friends.' It is crucial therefore, that the national list of gifted and talented children should include bright children from all social backgrounds, not just those from rich families.

I would bring some of the experiences from SIG and from the work of NAGTY to bear in developing provision for the future. Each secondary school should be required to appoint from its teaching staff a specialist counsellor for very able children to give general advice and support as well as counsel on which A-levels courses they should take and, if the school is an eleven-to-sixteen school, to which post-sixteen institutions their very able children should transfer. Some gifted children do not gain admittance to good universities because they receive poor advice on the best A-level subjects to take. For example, students seeking to study science at a leading university must study at least two science subjects at A-level as well as maths.

I know that it can sometimes be difficult for schools working in isolation to develop effective programmes, and able students benefit from being able to mix and compete with those of similar or higher ability. That is why I think it is important that schools work together to provide effective sixth-form challenge, and where schools don't currently have a sixth form, they consider ways to develop shared provision with other similar schools. One particularly effective example is provided by Carre's Grammar School and St George's Academy, which together have a joint sixth form in Sleaford, Lincolnshire. Provision of supplementary online courses for very able children, possibly by the Open University, should be offered. In the United States, the University of Missouri has made available a very effective online service. Perhaps the Open University would provide a similar service in the UK.

Most importantly of all, there should be clear accountability to judge whether or not the national gifted and talented programme is a success. Clearly the simplest and cheapest accountability would be to measure the proportion of those identified as gifted and talented who achieve three As at A-level or its equivalent and the proportion of these students who are admitted to a leading university. As the government now publishes university destination data, this should be a relatively simple matter to achieve.

The nurturing of our very able children is not only in this country's economic self-interest, but is also a matter of social justice to ensure that every child meets their potential. I hope that the current English Education Secretary, Michael Gove, will introduce an effective, high-quality gifted and talented programme in English schools.

My time at St Marylebone certainly helped me to get to Cambridge and I think that it is important that such opportunities are open to any able children. After I had left school – and had got my Cambridge place secured – it was time to embark on the rite of passage known as National Service, still a requirement for all young men in those days. Fourteen years after dodging the German warships to return from Africa to England, I would find myself back in the continent where I had been a toddler. This time it would be a very different experience.

4

KENYA & CAMBRIDGE

National Service in Kenya & Studying History at Cambridge

I was called up in March 1954 to do the two years of National Service required of every young British man in those days. I was quite excited at the prospect and looked forward to my two years in the Army. Basic training was with the Royal Army Pay Corps in the Wiltshire town of Devizes. We all lived in a big hut and the first morning in Devizes, I woke up to hear a Birmingham boy in the next bed asking me whether I had 'got a snout to lend me' – a popular slang term for a cigarette at the time. My sergeant encouraged me to apply for a commission which would allow me to train as an officer. I was still only eighteen and it was a pretty tough competition. Over two days of the test, we faced a heady mixture of giving speeches, intense physical activity and sports. The test was vigorous, with plenty of climbing over obstacle courses in order to determine if a candidate had leadership skills.

But I was fortunate enough to get through the War Office Selection Board (WOSB) – the seven others in my group didn't make it – though I still feel a twinge of terror when I recall my final interview. I had to march into the interview room and give my name and identification number. Fortunately, I did not stammer. Becoming an officer required another strenuous training regime, much of it at Eaton Hall in Chester, the home of the Duke of Westminster. Part of the training was to learn to climb a high fence with a backpack and a rifle. I struggled to do this, so threw my rifle over the fence. The watching officer said to the supervising trainer NCO, 'Take his name, Sergeant Major.' I was lucky to escape with a caution. Embedded in my mind still is the frightening battle camp training in the Welsh mountains at Trawsfynnedd, where we learned to attack positions with live ammunition and mortars. This was in the freezing depths of winter, with the ground covered in snow.

After being commissioned as a second lieutenant, towards the end of my training, I was asked to come in for a chat about my future assignment. They noted that I had been accepted by Cambridge University and had already learned French, Italian, Latin and Greek at school. Since they thought this would make me good material for the Intelligence Corps, they sent me down to London where I was quizzed me about my background. When my Whitehall interrogators seemed particularly keen that I should learn Russian, it became obvious that they wanted me to spend my time monitoring Soviet broadcasts. In effect, they wanted me to become a spy. Had I taken it further I might have found myself pursuing a very different career path. But I had no wish to become a secret agent. So, instead, I was given a commission in the East Surrey Regiment, based at Kingston, where I was granted a secondment to the King's African Rifles in Kenya during the Mau Mau emergency.

My eighteen months as the commander of Number 8 Platoon, C Company, in the 3rd Battalion of the King's African Rifles would prove to be a life-changing experience. I first had to learn Swahili, as my soldiers, who were warrior tribesmen from the Nandi, Kipsigis, Samburu, Wakamba and Somali tribes, did not speak English. Some of the troops had served in Burma against the Japanese and in Malaysia battling the Communist insurgents. They gave me a Swahili nickname of *bwana macho ine* – Master Four Eyes – because I wore glasses.

My company commander was Major Hugh Stockwell, a wise Second World War veteran. On my first evening with his company, he expressed concern that because of my missionary background, I would try to convert my soldiers to Christianity. I assured him that this was not part of my plan. He also advised me to listen to the sage advice of my platoon's warrant officer, platoon commander Mumo and his Samburu sergeant Laroi – the Samburu are relatives of the Masai. Both were experienced soldiers who had fought in Burma and Malaysia. They advised me not to lead patrols in the forest but to be third or fourth in line. This wise counsel saved my life when the leader of one of our patrols was killed by the Mau Mau.

Kenya in 1954 was experiencing the same rebellions against colonialism that characterised much of Africa over the next decade. Britain had already started to reduce the size of its empire, with India gaining independence in 1947 and many other colonies wanting to follow suit. But the conflict in Kenya which lasted between 1952 and 1960 was particularly bloody.

Many people believe that the Mau Mau were primarily a pro-independence movement of freedom fighters. However, they were mainly composed of extremist Kikuyu tribesmen and were not representative of the majority of Kenyans. Kenya has two major tribes: the Kikuyu and the Luo – President Obama's father was a Luo – and several smaller tribes, including the Masai, the Nandi, the Kipsigis, the Samburu, the Somali and the Wakamba. Only the Kikuyu supported the Mau Mau and that support was limited to a minority of the tribe.

Many of the Mau Mau activists lived on the Aberdare highlands where most of the land was occupied by the white settlers. Seizing their land was as important an objective for many Mau Mau fighters as independence. Impoverished Kikuyu villagers looked with envy on the rich farmlands occupied by the whites, though many of them did not support the Mau Mau. Recent evidence has come to light of some of the torture and terrible treatment that some Kenyans received during the suppression of the Mau Mau, and I hope that they will receive justice. But it is also important to remember the appalling nature of the atrocities committed by the Mau Mau. One famous case involved Arundell Gray Leakey, the cousin of the famous archaeologist Louis Leakey, who was brutally disembowelled and buried upside down, alive, on Mount Kenya. It is also worth noting that the father of modern Kenya, the Kikuyu leader Jomo Kenyatta, did not support the Mau Mau nor did they enjoy support from other key tribesmen. Indeed it was only when the Mau Mau were defeated in 1960 that sensible discussions could take place on independence that allowed the new Kenya to be born in December 1963.

But that was a long way from the experience of patrolling the Aberdare Mountains and Mount Kenya forest from 1954 to 1956. Our mission was to search for Mau Mau, especially in the forests near Nyeri, including in areas close to the Tree Tops hotel where the then Princess Elizabeth had been told of her father's death in 1952, and on the slopes of Mount Kenya near Naro Moru and Nanyuki. If proof were needed of the limited support that the Mau Mau had even within their own tribe, my platoon developed good relations with many Kikuyu villagers, who were often only too happy to reveal where the Mau Mau were hiding.

Yet, it was a dangerous mission and we were involved in several nasty skirmishes. After one encounter, the Mau Mau ran away except for one man who climbed a tree. My soldiers wanted to shoot him. I ordered them not to do so but to take him prisoner. We obtained very useful information from him.

Typically my platoon of thirty-five soldiers would patrol the forest and mountains for a month at a time, receiving our rations in very welcome air drops. The extremely rugged terrain often involved climbing to heights of several thousand feet. Each soldier, myself included, had to carry a rucksack with a small tent, enough food and 100 rounds of ammunition. It was here, too, that I learned to use a compass to determine where I was in the forest by taking back bearings from mountaintops. This was particularly important, since each platoon had a specific area to patrol. For someone not yet nineteen years of age to be put nominally in charge of so many fierce African warriors, some of whom had seen active service in Burma and Malaysia, was a daunting experience. But it was also truly life-changing. I learned a great deal, including the importance of listening to those who knew better and the importance of camaraderie.

Wild animals had been the bane of my childhood gardening efforts in the Congo. Here in Kenya they were rather more dangerous. Elephants, rhinos and buffaloes may look attractive from the safety of a safari Jeep or a tourist coach, but it is a different matter when you are patrolling their terrain. Early in my service, my platoon was charged by a fierce rhino in the Aberdare Mountains. In the chaos that followed, one of the soldiers accidentally shot and killed the platoon sergeant. It was a terrible tragedy.

Set against that, some of our other problems were more mundane, though they felt rather more challenging at the time. Hygiene is never easy in the wild, and to use the toilet, we had to dig a hole in the forest. Of course, this meant that former camps were not always particularly sanitary. One day when searching for a new camp site, we came across a former army site in the forest with an old fence around it. My soldiers wanted to camp there but I was worried by the possible hygiene problems. Refusing to agree to use the site caused a near mutiny among the soldiers, though I was fortunate that Warrant Officer Mumo supported me. So we waited patiently for the soldiers to agree we should find another site. I like to think that in doing so, I saved them from some nasty diseases. Finding suitable camp sites was always a challenge. On another occasion, we unwisely pitched camp on a route elephants took to drink water in the nearby river. We had to leave in a panic in the middle of the night when we heard the elephants coming towards us.

One of the huge advantages of serving with local Kenyan solders in the forest was that they always knew the way back to camp. Their sense of direction and knowledge of their country was a lot better than that of the wholly British regiments, who frequently got lost in the forest and strayed into our assigned area. When this happened, it caused much concern to my African soldiers, who feared that the English solders would think they were Mau Mau because they were black.

Even though I was still a teenager, I think I earned the respect of the Kenyan soldiers in my platoon. I took the time to learn Swahili, and I am still fluent in the language. I felt particularly honoured to be invited to join the *Motoyawezei* (a Swahili term for the camp fire of the older and wiser soldiers). I also ate African rations, which were much tastier than the meagre white officers' food that came in small tin cans. In the evenings, the senior soldiers would tell stories of their tribes and previous service. The camaraderie was extraordinary. One of my soldiers saved my life by pulling me out of a swamp into which I had fallen running away from a charging buffalo. He risked his life in the process by climbing precariously onto an overhanging tree to haul me out. I am forever in his debt.

We were able to take leave twice a year. This gave me the chance to experience something of the beauty of the continent that I had briefly glimpsed on the journey back to England in 1940. I sailed around Lake Victoria on a fishing boat and visited the city of Mombasa. But the most exciting place I visited was the island of Zanzibar, with its toxic mix of Arabic, Persian and Portuguese culture, and the presence of wonderful spices in the markets of the capital city. The people, who are largely Muslim, speak Swahili, so my linguistic learning came in handy.

There was time for sport too, and I played rugby for the 3rd King's African Rifles against the 4th KAR (the Ugandan Battalion). But not all encounters on the sporting field were pleasant ones. As a wing, I was tackled brutally by a huge Ugandan forward. I was on the verge of scoring a try, when suddenly he walloped me from nowhere. When I got up, somewhat shaken, I asked my team mates, 'Who the hell was that?' 'Oh, his name is Sergeant Idi Amin,' they replied. I had been rugby tackled by the man later to become the infamous President of Uganda. In retrospect, I probably got off lightly.

The Army asked me to remain in post with a permanent commission when my National Service ended in March 1956. But I was keen to take up my place at Cambridge, so I declined their offer. But I left Kenya with a rich mix of experiences and thoughts. I can never forget what a gloriously beautiful country Kenya is, with the resources to become a wealthy country, although too often it suffers from drought. Kenyan independence in 1963 was a time of real hope. The country has enjoyed phases of real success, and Nairobi remains an important financial centre. But it has never achieved its full potential as a result of tribal conflicts that have prevented the many able Kenyans from working together to advance their country. These conflicts came to a head after a close election in 2007, when 1,000 people died in ethnic conflicts. A new constitution in 2010 heralded new hope for the country, and I hope that it helps this wonderful country to thrive again.

Cambridge Years

After I left Kenya and the Army in March 1956, I returned to England to live with my sisters Sylvia and Wendy who were by this time living in Chelsea. With six months before I had to go up to Cambridge in October, I took a job as a teacher for a term at a private boarding preparatory school called Streete Court, which was located near Godstone in Surrey. I enjoyed teaching the children, most of whom were from other countries, but not working for the headmaster, who I felt to be a bit of a tyrant. Once school had broken up, I still had a few months to wait, so Sylvia got me a job in a restaurant on the King's Road in Chelsea. This may have been a few years before the Swinging Sixties made the King's Road famous. Nevertheless, I had a great time learning several different roles in the La Reve, which was run by a Mr Gorman. I took turns on the till, serving wine and operating the all-important coffee machine. The experience also provided an object lesson in human relations, as the brilliant French chef played up to his temperamental stereotype and enjoyed relations with the other staff that could only be described as difficult.

But these were just interludes before Cambridge. Come October 1956, I was delighted finally to be able to take up my place at Trinity Hall, where I was to read History for the next three years. Trinity Hall was founded by Bishop Bateman of Norwich in 1350, in a bid, it is said, to replenish a priesthood that was devastated by the Black Death. It is a smaller college than its neighbours, and is best known for teaching the law. It was where my father had studied before he left for the Congo. As Stacey had also been there, I was following a family tradition.

I shared a room with Alan Moller who had also been in the King's African Rifles and subsequently, on graduation, had a distinguished career in the British Council. Our next door neighbours included Mark Tully, later the voice of the BBC in India, and Parvez Radji, an Iranian with close links to the Shah of Persia, who became the Iranian Ambassador to London and Rome. Mark and I were founder members of the infamous Silver Crab Club, a dining and drinking club of amateur oarsmen, and we held some pretty wild parties. Rowing was a very important sport. Instead of having regular races, we had 'bump races' where we had to bump the boat in front of us. It required heroic effort to avoid being bumped. We had also bought an old punt for £14 (£275 at today's prices) which we called the *Ying Tong* after the popular song Spike Milligan wrote for *The Goon Show*. After one of our drinking parties, which went on well beyond the 10 p.m. curfew, Mark was rather the worse for wear. After the doors were shut, latecomers faced a fine, and Mark had no wish to pay this penalty. So he decided to scale the 10-foot wall, but he fell on one of the spikes and was quite badly hurt, though luckily there were no lasting scars.

But Trinity Hall in 1956 was a very male, elitist institution. I was conscious that I was one of a very few grammar school boys at the college, and had not been to the leading public schools that many of my fellow undergraduates had attended. Indeed the vast majority of its students were then from this background. Today the college admits women and is more diverse. But at the time, there was a degree of snobbery which meant that I sometimes felt that I wasn't accepted on the same terms as other students. A small example was that I was not invited to join the Asparagus Club, the well-known dining club, then dominated by public schoolboys. Nevertheless, I did make some close friends, including Alan Moller, Philip Gaussen, John Rose, Chris Lindholmes, Edward Stanford, Graham Ross Russell and Miles Halford, some of whom I still see today. The all-male college didn't prevent me from dating either and I preferred going out with the European girls attending the English language schools in Cambridge – after all, there were only three female colleges at Cambridge at that time.

I was determined to make the most of my Cambridge experience, and was helped in no small measure by having some excellent history tutors, notably Geoffrey Best and Charles Crawley, who had also taught my brother Stacey. But I owe the most to my personal tutor, Revd Robert Runcie, who later became Archbishop of Canterbury. He gave me wise advice such as not to drink too much – given that on one occasion, two particularly drunk members of our group collapsed outside his door, I know this was heartfelt – but more importantly, he encouraged and supported my application to Harvard Business School. Robert Runcie also effected another introduction later in life when he was the Archbishop and recommended me to the Prime Minister Margaret Thatcher. In two very important ways, and at two different times, he would change the course of my life.

It was a real privilege being at Cambridge, as we enjoyed some unparalleled teaching experiences. Most of the teaching was centred on weekly independent meetings with tutors during which we as students read out an essay. We were also expected to read widely, a habit I have tried to maintain. By contrast, the history lectures, which should have been well attended, were often half-empty as many students only attended sporadically as they were not required to do so.

The long summer holidays at British universities have their benefits. We could take a vacation from the middle of May to the middle of October, and these five month breaks provided excellent opportunities to explore the world. In 1956 before going to Cambridge, I enjoyed a wonderful visit to Spain with a fellow teacher from the Streete Court School, taking in the Prado in Madrid and Toledo, culminating in ten days in the Costa Brava September sunshine at Tossa del Mar – in the days before package holidays. I'm afraid to say – as a contemporary letter home to Mother records – that between five-course meals and wine at a local pension, where we paid just 17/6d (£17 at today's prices) for full board, a group of us would lie on the beach and tease other nationalities. This teasing culminated in our swimming out at three in the morning to plant the Spanish flag on a rock half a mile out to sea, to the bemusement of the locals the next morning. Despite such juvenile japes, I found the Spanish people delightful, and loved hearing Bach and Handel in the local church by night in the company of many tourists from France, Germany and America. But that was a mere taster for what I would do in 1957, the year I started a relationship with America that was to last to this day.

5

CROSSING THE ATLANTIC

Harvard Business School, Working at Procter &
Gamble & Travelling in America in the 1950s

My first visit to America involved a degree of enterprise. I was asked by Miles Halford, my friend at Cambridge, to help him to charter a propeller-driven DC6 aeroplane to fly fellow students who wanted to work in the summer in the United States to New York. This was my first entrepreneurial adventure. It was successful as every seat was sold, and of course, Miles and I flew free of charge. It was also my first time in America, and the start of a lifelong love affair with this remarkable country.

In that summer of '57, once we had landed in New York – after a sixteen-hour obligatory stopover in Gander Airport, Newfoundland – and safely dispatched our passengers, we stayed with my sister Mary in the city. Coming from a still staid England, I was astonished to find shops and the subway open all night and cinemas where the last movie started at 2.30 in the morning. With Edward Stanford, who had also joined us on the trip, we drove an American millionaire's Cadillac from New York City to Niagara. Calvin Rand had needed someone to bring one of his three cars to his summer retreat in Canada. We were put up for the night in his seven-bedroomed retreat – formerly the residence of the local Governor.

I then hitch-hiked to stay with my brother, who was by now living in Canada. Stacey – or the Revd Eustace Lovett Hebden Taylor as he was now known – was the Anglican vicar at the Holy Trinity Church in Témiscaming, Quebec. I told Mother in a letter at the time that my brother's house was 'a wonderful combination of Bohemianism, wonderful books, good food, Taylor humour and babies' nappies'. I was also fascinated that his car was an automatic. The small town was dominated by the paper mills, and while there, I got a job paying $1.80 an hour as a blow pit operator with the Canadian International Paper

Company. This involved me squirting a high-pressure hosepipe into a large underground cavern to wash out the pulp. When the cavern was empty, I had to carefully manoeuvre the wooden lid back into place, so that the cellar could be refilled. I watched my experienced fellow French Canadian workers casually kick their lids into place. One day I decided to try this too. Inevitably the lid crashed through the opening into the cellar 50 feet below. I thought I would be fired on the spot, but the foreman simply smiled and said, 'Every guy gets one turn.'

After working there for the summer and earning quite a lot of cash, I joined Miles and Edward Stanford in Chicago, where we bought an old car and we drove to the West Coast to San Francisco, and back. It was an amazing trip, but it was not without its hazards. We crashed into another car in Chicago when it stopped suddenly in front of us, and nearly fell over a 10,000-foot drop when our brakes failed in the Yosemite Pass in California. As we slept in the Yellowstone Park, grizzly bears broke into our ice box a few feet from our tents. I was also stopped for speeding in Atlanta. But these were small trials on a great trip. Nothing could stop us appreciating the magnificence of the giant redwoods that adorn the incredible Yosemite national park. We went to New Orleans to enjoy the music where I couldn't believe the amount of jazz oozing out from dozens of different clubs. I reported home from Las Vegas in September 1957 that I was 'sitting in a frenzied gambling den at half past one in the morning', though I think that was little more than youthful bravado.

At the end of the trip I visited Harvard Business School on the recommendation of my foreman at the pulp mill in Canada, who was himself a graduate of the school. The admissions dean who interviewed me said that because of my interesting background, I would likely be accepted if I applied to join the MBA programme. I was determined to do this, but I would need to save a lot of money to pay the high fees. So, the next summer, in 1958, I managed to get a reasonably well-paid job as the camp organiser at a fruit farm in Cambridgeshire, supervising some fifty foreign student fruit pickers. Though quite a challenge, it gave me a lot of the money I needed though not yet enough.

After graduating with second-class honours from Cambridge in May 1959, I was accepted by Harvard Business School. But before I started, I still needed to earn enough to pay for my fees and keep while there. In the summer of 1959, I worked as a courier with Blue Cars, taking groups of British and American tourists round Europe. The bus trips took in a lot over ten days, often covering Paris, Geneva, Florence, Rome and parts of Germany. As a courier, I had to run the whole tour, and this was when I really learned the travel business, as well as earning considerable sums from tips and the optional tours I sold to my passengers. I could also earn commissions by negotiating discounts with shops en route, particularly Swiss watchmakers.

An experienced fellow courier, Jimmy Coronna, was my great mentor at this time, and he would subsequently become the travel director of the American Institute for Foreign Study five years later. Without Jimmy's help, AIFS would have never survived its first year. For now, I was grateful to him for showing me the ropes so well. I worked with Blue Cars in the summers of 1960 and 1961 too. Besides earning a lot of money, I learned how important great service is to a successful travel business.

1959–61: Harvard Business School

I arrived at Harvard Business School in September 1959 late at night from Montreal, having taken a transatlantic voyage to the Canadian city on a student ship. I was too tired from my journey to appreciate my surroundings. But there would be little respite before I had to knuckle down to work. The Business School had been founded in 1908 to teach graduates of the prestigious – and much older – university the rudiments of business. Located across the river from the main campus, the Business School is closer to the bustle of Boston. The two-year MBA programme was very challenging from the start. For example, it was the practice to start the first lesson of the first year with a 100-page case study used in the previous first year's final examination. In my first lesson in marketing, given by Milton P. Brown, a famous HBS professor who remained close to the School until his death in 2009, I was stunned when the professor cold-called a student sitting next to me to start the discussion. To my amazement, my neighbour talked with authority for several minutes on the case, despite its length. At that moment, I was convinced that the admissions dean had made a big mistake by giving me a place. I had barely read the case script.

All the teaching was based on case studies, and we reviewed three cases – many of them fifty pages long – every day. With my British friends, including Bruno Schroder, Paul Mortimer and Graham Ross-Russell, I quickly learned that the trick was to study one case a day very thoroughly, while skim-reading the other two. You would then volunteer to speak in the discussion of the case you had studied well. Professors soon grew tired of me spouting on those cases and did not bother to call me on those I had merely skim-read. Days felt long too after the relatively relaxed atmosphere of Cambridge, where I regarded four hours as hard work: lectures ran from 8.40 to 2.30 and we were expected to spend at least four more hours preparing for the next day's discussions and interrogations.

It was also the practice for new students to take a reading test upon arrival. My test showed that I was a slow reader and that slow readers do not understand the meaning of the words they are reading as well as fast readers. They enrolled me in an Evelyn Wood Rapid Reading Course which doubled my rate of reading as well as improving my understanding. This has proved to be invaluable over the years. I also found myself at a bit of a disadvantage when I started because, unlike most of my classmates, I had neither a technical nor an accounting background, and needed to work harder to keep up with them.

The Harvard course covered production, marketing, finance, accounting, administration, report writing and business economics. So much was drummed into us in the first months that I reported home to Mother in March 1960 that we were 'practically walking business manuals'. The level of competition was also extraordinary. We all knew each other's views on all the topics that we had to discuss. But it was also very dangerous to open one's mouth without being absolutely sure – or at least convinced – about the truth or validity of what one was saying. We had three-hour examinations every Saturday morning in one of our subjects, usually involving solving a real-life business problem.

Despite the slightly terrifying start, I made friends and was enjoying myself after the first couple of months. But studying at Harvard was not just incredibly demanding, it was also expensive, and I ran out of funds at the end of my first year, despite my summer work as a Blue Cars courier. For some months, I was convinced that I wouldn't be able to afford the second year. So I was very grateful to receive the very generous Charles Bell Scholarship from the London Chamber of Commerce worth £500 – or £9,500 at today's prices. Along with two other students, I also got the school newspaper concession during my second year. One of my partners was Dominic Paino, an extraordinary salesman. We persuaded the older executive students to buy lots of papers, which meant that we had to get up every morning at 6 a.m. to deliver newspapers to 1,000 students. However, we each earned a substantial sum, and together with the scholarship and a student loan, I could now afford the fees and living costs.

In my second year, I majored in Entrepreneurial Studies and prepared a paper on how to start a travel business, drawing on my Blue Cars experience. I also added Advanced Economic Analysis to the usual five courses. My grades in my second year were also better than in the first year. I was now earning more and I could even afford to buy my first car – a good second-hand Ford – for only $300 from a fellow student. Despite having money in my pocket, however, I had had little time for much social activity at HBS, though I did date a lovely young lady who came from a famous aristocratic Boston family living in Louisburg Square. I was pleased to graduate in the top third of the class of 1,000 students in 1961.

As I had very much enjoyed my time at Harvard Business School, I decided to live and work permanently in the US after graduation to put some of the ideas I had learned into practice by emigrating to the United States. I was able to do this easily because I had got a Green Card before I left England, and this gave me permanent residence rights. I had already spent two years studying at Harvard, but this felt more like a decision to emigrate. With my Harvard MBA under my belt, I applied for several jobs and was fortunate to be offered a position in the marketing department of Procter & Gamble in Cincinnati, Ohio. William Procter, an English candle maker, and James Gamble, an Irish soap maker, had founded the company in Cincinnati in 1837 and its soaps had become an American mainstay during the nineteenth century. By 1961 it was a major multinational and was about to launch a product that would revolutionise many mothers' lives: the disposable nappy.

But at the interview, my interviewer seemed more concerned to know why I was not applying to work for the company in England. Ever modest, I replied that I wanted to be president of P & G Worldwide. This ambition impressed him and he promptly offered me a job at the Cincinnati headquarters.

1961–64: Procter & Gamble

I drove my precious Ford the 900 miles from the Harvard campus in Cambridge, Massachusetts to Cincinnati, towing a U-Haul with all my worldly possessions behind it along the Interstate 70 highway. My ambitions might have been high, but I had to start as a staff assistant in the Marketing Department working in the bullpen, a large area where all junior staff worked. Since I didn't like working in the bullpen, this motivated me to work hard for promotion so I could get my own office.

My first assignment that September was working on Liquid Prell, a shampoo which rivalled Head and Shoulders as America's best-selling brand in the 1950s. The green liquid had been sold to women as the shampoo that would provide 'that radiantly alive look'. My job involved thinking of new ways to promote the brand and liaising with the New York advertising agency to plan copy and media decisions for the multi-million dollar marketing budget. Despite my Cambridge and Harvard training, I also had to learn to write the P & G way, sometimes having to rewrite memos ten times until they were just right. No statement or recommendation could be made without the facts to back them up. Everything was analysed numerically, although there was opportunity for original thinking. Facts and evidence have always been important to me since.

After six months, I went on sales training to Kansas City where I lived in the Plaza area. I was made responsible for a regular sales district covering Kansas and Iowa for the P & G toilet goods division – each division had its own specialist sales force. I introduced myself as an exchange salesman from England and was able to obtain some substantial orders. Spending four months selling to supermarkets and drug stores taught me the basic skills of communication, which were to prove invaluable in later life.

Although I was in America, there was still a chance to play cricket, and I played for the local Kansas team made up mainly of Indian and British emigrants like myself. We played in the public park and in away matches in St Louis and at the main University of Kansas campus in Lawrence. While in Kansas, we also had the chance to take in more of the country on vacation. Roy Pfeil, a friend from Cincinnati, and I drove the old Ford to Aspen, in Colorado, which was only just becoming an important ski resort in those days. We camped in the Rockies one night, waking up to find we were in several inches of snow, and we had incredible difficulty driving the car down again. We then drove to the amazing Grand Canyon, which is the most incredible physical sight I have seen in my life. This vast gorge, which represents 2 billion years of geological history, is 277 miles long, up to 18 miles wide and over a mile deep. It simply takes your breath away. We wanted to do more than see what most tourists saw from the top, so we climbed down on foot and slept in the Ranch by the Colorado Riverside. After two days there, the climb back up was not quite so easy.

I returned to Cincinnati after four months in Kansas. Home in Cincinnati was a charming but small two-room apartment at 959 Hill Street, overlooking the Ohio River. The apartment was in the oldest part of town, Mount Adams, a German district regarded as the arty quarter. My neighbours were young bachelors who were constantly throwing exciting parties. I also used my English accent to get invited to the exciting débutante parties given by the wealthy Cincinnati families for their daughters at local country clubs.

One of the challenges of working as a brand manager was developing a productive relationship with your advertising agency.

I worked with Benton & Bowles in New York and Tate & Laird in Chicago. My recollections of dealing with the creative advertisers are not at all like the lifestyle portrayed in the *Mad Men* TV series. Our advertising agencies, possibly because they were dealing with such an important client as Procter & Gamble, were older people who treated us with great respect. There was far more partying in my Cincinnati neighbourhood than in their New York and Chicago offices.

At Procter & Gamble, I worked on several different brands over the coming months. Some had a greater appeal than others. Lilt Homeware had one big advantage: it was the sponsor of the Miss Universe beauty pageant, which was still a popular mainstream event in those days. Drug stores would have to buy several cases of the product if they were to receive life-size display boards of the contestants, which they all wanted to display. As part of the promotion, I was expected to spend several days in Miami where the contest was held. I was in the hotel where all the contestants stayed, and was astonished to see a naked woman in one of the corridors, coming out of one of the bedrooms. Naturally, as a chivalrous Englishman, I took my coat off and gave it to her to cover herself. She explained that she was a Norwegian contestant, and she had had a terrible row with her room-mate, and had been kicked out. I was happy to come to her aid. Such were the responsibilities of the P & G marketing man. I was less keen to be working on the Secret deodorant account. Although the work was interesting, I was ashamed to tell my friends what I was promoting.

I later transferred to Gleam toothpaste, the third-largest-selling US toothpaste after Crest and Colgate, which had annual sales of almost $1 billion. My great coup was to persuade senior P & G managers in 1964 to buy 1 million tubes of Play-Doh, a modelling compound popular with young children, to put on the tubes of Gleam as a promotion in the supermarkets and shops. Normally, promotions of this sort would first be test-marketed, but I told P & G managers that Colgate would buy the Play-Doh if Gleam did not do so immediately.

My brand manager, Mike Levine, was a fairly demanding character – he would ask to see me if I turned up two minutes late in the morning. He also taught me a lot. Every Friday afternoon, he would make me produce a list of what I planned to do in the next week, and to detail it by order of priority. The following Friday we would review what I had accomplished. That taught me priorities. So, it was not insignificant when Mike told me I was putting my career at risk by going ahead with the promotion without a test market. But P & G products are judged by their market share. The Play-Doh promotion increased Gleam's share of the total toothpaste market, in the Nielsen ratings, from 17 to 19 per cent, an amazing increase in the multi-billion dollar toothpaste market. Even Mike had to concede I had backed a winner, and my success came to the attention of the P & G toilet goods general manager, Bill Snow, who congratulated me and told me my future at P & G was assured. But my life was about to change in two hugely important ways.

6

THE AIFS STORY

The History of the American Institute for Foreign Study

It was at this time that I fell in love with Judy Denman, a beautiful French language teacher at Glen Este High School, who had been a student at Radcliffe, a Harvard college. I first met Judy at a Cincinnati débutante party and was much impressed by her beauty and intelligence. We got married in Cincinnati and will celebrate our fiftieth wedding anniversary in 2015.

I had benefited from the chance to study in America, and felt that there should be more opportunities for people from different countries to study and spend time with each other. But it was when Judy had difficulties organising an educational trip for her pupils to France, to learn French, that the idea of the American Institute for Foreign Study was born. When she applied to the Foreign Language League, a Mormon organisation in Salt Lake City run by the Debry family – at the time the only programme offering such trips for US high school students – she discovered that they were full.

So, Judy asked if I could organise an itinerary, drawing on my Blue Cars experience. I arranged a programme in La Rochelle on the Atlantic coast of France, but her students were unable to raise the necessary funds. They had tried to raise money by selling chocolate to their fellow students, but the produce had proved rather too tempting. They had eaten most of the chocolate themselves rather than selling it.

However, the experience set me thinking. There was clearly an untapped market for such school trips abroad led by teachers. So I spent my two-week Procter & Gamble summer vacation in August 1964 setting up summer study abroad programmes for high school students at universities in Madrid and Salamanca, in Spain, La Rochelle, Tours, St Malo and Vichy in France, Perugia in Italy and

Salzburg in Austria. I left P & G in September 1964 to focus on the new enterprise. With Roger Walther and Doug Burck, two other young brand managers, AIFS was born that September with my Hill Street apartment as its world headquarters.

I was able to bring all the skills and contacts I had developed to good use. One of the advertising agencies I worked with purchased a list of 25,000 US high school modern language teachers for us and we offered these teachers a free trip if they recruited eight students on our programme. A typical four-week AIFS study programme in 1965 at a university, including airfare and travel, cost $685 (or $5,000 at today's prices).

We had clearly tapped into a demand that was not being met. Our student groups in the first summer in 1965 went to seven European universities: Salamanca, Madrid, Perugia, Tours, La Rochelle, Vichy and Salzburg. Large groups were organised by Nell Khady at Needham Broughton School in Raleigh, North Carolina to go to La Rochelle, and Janet Nevius from Monclair High School, New Jersey to Tours. We opened an office in the Temple Bar Building in Cincinnati, and engaged several staff. During the first summer of 1965, 1,500 students and teachers participated, paying AIFS $1 million in tuition fees. Fortunately my partner, Roger Walther, negotiated a line of credit of $25,000 with the Putnam Trust Bank in Greenwich in May 1965 when we still had $1 million in the bank, as after we had paid the bills of the first summer, we were out of funds. That loan kept us in business. An important business lesson that I always remembered is to negotiate a loan before you actually need the money.

A year after its launch, AIFS moved its offices to Greenwich, Connecticut to be closer to the New York airports from which charter flights run by Saturn, Capitol and Trans International Airlines departed. It was time for us to leave Cincinnati too. Judy and I moved to a garage apartment in Round Hill, in Greenwich, where she took on a new teaching job. Our garage apartment was rented from Otto Fuerbringer, then editor of *Time* magazine.

Expanding AIFS with Robert Kennedy's Help

From 1965 to 1968, the high school programme grew rapidly to nearly 5,000 students with many new summer campuses being opened including in England at such prestigious universities as St Andrew's, Durham, Exeter, Bangor, Norwich and even Oxford and Cambridge. In 1968, AIFS started its second major programme: study abroad for college students, both in the summer and year round. The first full-time semester programmes were opened in Salamanca, Perugia, Salzburg and Grenoble.

Following a private dinner in 1967 with Senator Jacob Javitz of New York hosted by my landlord Otto Fuerbringer, the *Time* editor, at his house we agreed to offer scholarships on the AIFS high school programme to students recommended by Senators Javitz and Robert Kennedy, and by Mayor John Lindsay of New York. Javitz and Lindsay nominated a candidate each. But Senator Kennedy was much more ambitious: he mailed several schools in disadvantaged areas of New York City, inviting them to nominate candidates. Perhaps not surprisingly, a large number of students applied for a scholarship. He was invited to interview them, but said he wanted all of them to be given scholarships and would raise the funds. One of Kennedy's staff called me to ask if AIFS was a registered US charity. I replied that we were not. Senator Kennedy then recommended that we set up a foundation, and do so within the three weeks before the students were supposed to leave. The wheels of bureaucracy did not usually grind so quickly. However, after applying to the Internal Revenue Service, a tax official called from their Hartford office within a few days asking for details. He told me that 'he did not want to keep the good Senator waiting'. I was amazed. I went to see Senator Kennedy in his apartment overlooking the United Nations Building in New York. He asked me what the children would actually learn. When I explained that they would learn a foreign language and have a life-changing experience in Europe, he seemed satisfied that it would be a worthwhile activity. As a direct result of his intervention, over 1,000 children have benefited over the years from both Europe and the United States. Sadly it would be less than a year before the gifted presidential candidate was gunned down by an assassin in Los Angeles. He was a seriously impressive figure. What a shame he did not live to be president.

But Robert Kennedy's legacy lives on. Thanks to his intervention, the AIFS Foundation has been a major provider of funds for scholarships to disadvantaged young people for study abroad as well as organising its own programmes. And we have retained links with the Kennedy family, particularly with his daughter Kathleen Kennedy Townsend, as well as more recently his widow Ethel Kennedy. Ben Davenport has been its chairman since 1971. Ben, a gifted educator in the Greenwich school system, was one of our first principals to lead summer schools in the UK starting with the University of Exeter in 1967.

Since 1978, the AIFS Foundation has been authorised by the US State Department under the J visa programme to organise its Academic Year in America programme for foreign high school students to spend a year staying with a US family while attending the local high school. Such links do an enormous amount to open young people's horizons and make the world a smaller place.

AIFS in the 1970s and Beyond

With a thriving business, the three AIFS shareholders decided in 1969, perhaps unwisely, to sell the company to National Student Marketing Corporation (NSMC) for $1 million each plus shares in NSMC, though we had to stay on to run the company. The Chairman of NSMC, Cortes Randell, was subsequently convicted of fraud. Fortunately AIFS was able to buy itself back from NSMC in 1977, as it had gone public in the intervening period. One positive benefit of that unfortunate experience was that we acquired Camp America, originally called Rural Britannia, from NSMC. Through Camp America, we brought thousands of British and other foreign students to work as camp counsellors during the summer in the US, and arranged for them to have J visas. One of the many young people to benefit was the polar explorer David Hempleman-Adams, who spent three summers with Camp America. He says the experience taught him 'many things including how to take responsibility for one's life and to get on with people from different backgrounds'. He adds that 'these qualities proved invaluable in my career as an explorer and a mountaineer'.

He is not alone. Camp America had a peak enrolment by 2001 of nearly 10,000 students. I am always heartened by the continuing popularity of the programme when I visit our annual camp fairs at Kensington Town Hall, in London, where up to 3,000 young people turn up seeking a Camp America role. They are interviewed on the spot for what can be a very demanding job for the eight to ten weeks they are in the United States. Because the Town Hall can only accommodate 1,000 young people, the queues often extend well down the street outside. Sir Alec Reed, the founder of Reed Employment, one of the largest recruitment agencies in Europe, told me that if an employer saw Camp America on an applicant's CV, they would be much more likely to hire them.

Douglas Burck left the company in 1970 to join the Peace Corps in Peru, though fortunately, Roger Walther, my other wonderful partner and a genius at doing deals, remained as a key figure in AIFS. In the same year we felt that we needed to open a satellite office in London and it was agreed that I move to London to supervise the overseas operations at the AIFS office at 10 Kendrick Place in Kensington. However I kept our home in Greenwich, Connecticut and my wife and I frequently returned to the United States. My Green Card was renewed every ten years. Our daughter, Livia Kirsten Hebden Taylor, had been born just months before on 17 February 1970 in Brooklyn Hospital, New York.

The 1970s saw substantial growth as the AIFS college division increased programme offerings to Europe, Africa, Asia and South America and expanded Richmond College, which became a university. In 1971, wishing to offer its own study abroad programme in London, AIFS purchased Richmond College on Richmond Hill in Richmond, Surrey, an outer London borough. Richmond College eventually became the American International University in London – about which there is more in the next chapter. In 1974, we moved from Kendrick Place to 37 Queen's Gate in Kensington SW7, which continues to operate as the UK headquarters of AIFS with the later addition of 38 Queen's Gate next door, rented from the Ghanaian High Commission.

Our College Division continued to expand in the 1980s. In addition to summer, semester and academic year programmes, we established a new type of study abroad programme. Partnership Programs, headed by Ailsa Brookes, enabled colleges and universities to create their own customised programmes and bring faculty abroad. This proved a popular option for community college students seeking a low-cost study abroad alternative.

In 1986, we also embarked on a programme to make it easier for young women to become au pairs in America. Young women were authorised to come to the United States to work on an official J visa with private families, providing childcare to US families while studying part-time. The programme was an instant success, but its growth in the nineties owed much to Senator Jesse Helms of North Carolina, at that time Chairman of the Senate Foreign Relations Committee, who was able to gain permanent authorisation for the programme following a special Act of Congress in 1997. Without the support of Senator Helms, we would never have got this crucial Act. It was signed into statute by President Clinton. The programme started with just 475 participants in 1986 and now has 13,000 participants a year.

The Au Pair programme has promoted nearly 100,000 cultural and childcare exchange opportunities with professional families in the US and given thousands of young women from over sixty countries the chance to study and work in America. While the programme started in England, it was affected for a time by the publicity surrounding the case of Louise Woodward, a nineteen-year-old English au pair with no connection to our programme, who was convicted of the involuntary manslaughter of an eight-month-old baby in her care in Massachusetts in 1997. The numbers of English au pairs declined as a result. There are now far more young women from Germany on the programme, where they have the driving and English-speaking skills required. They see it like a gap year. I hope that more young English women will see the benefits of the programme, particularly at a time when internships and jobs for young people are so much in demand.

AIFS acquired two other cultural exchange companies, ELS (English Language Services) and the American Council for International Studies (ACIS), an educational high school company, in 1987, after which ACIS merged with the AIFS high school division to form a joint high school operation based in Boston, Massachusetts. Enrolment for the combined high school programme reached a peak of 31,300 participants in 2001.

AIFS became a public company listed on the American Stock Exchange in 1986 but I later re-acquired it with Roger Walther in 1990. In 1993 my partner Roger wished to concentrate on other business ventures on the West Coast so we split AIFS, with the ELS division becoming a separate company under Roger's direction in San Francisco. By that stage, ELS had become one of the largest English language programmes in the United States, with a peak enrolment while owned by AIFS of over 31,000 participants in 1992. Taken together, there were 66,000 AIFS participants that year, making it one of the largest such programmes in the world.

The 1990s were excellent years for AIFS as study abroad continued to grow in popularity. Programmes were organised in Australia and South Africa by Mark Simpson and we offered an internship option at Richmond. The internet was a big factor in our expansion, backed by strong marketing campaigns and increasing awareness in international programmes. Au Pair and Camp America continued to thrive due to tremendous efforts by our incredibly professional staff, including Ruth Ferry at Au Pair and Dennis Regan and Janet Henniker-Talle at Camp America.

In 1992, AIFS created Cultural Insurance Services International (CISI), now led by Linda Langin, to offer insurance to its students. It soon became popular with other study abroad providers as well as universities and colleges offering study abroad programmes. An international insurance company called CareMed in Germany was later acquired in this decade by AIFS to service international clients. In 1994 the AIFS Board decided that the future prospects for Richmond University would be enhanced if it became independent of AIFS with formal US 501 (c) (3) charitable status. However, AIFS continues to retain ownership of the buildings which Richmond occupies and AIFS continues to recruit study abroad students in the US for the Richmond programmes in London, Florence and Rome.

In the late 1990s, AIFS acquired GIJK in Bonn, Germany (now known as AIFS Deutschland), led by Thomas Kiechle, and Au Pair Discover in South Africa to market its Au Pair, Camp America and Academic Year in America programmes. AIFS also established a Resort America programme to assist US resorts with their international staffing needs and provide cultural exchanges. We established branch offices in Sydney, Australia led by Wendi Aylward and in Warsaw, Poland led by Michal Pagowski. The growing size of the global operation also saw its US operation move within Connecticut from Greenwich, where it had been based since the sixties, to Stamford.

In June 2000 AIFS acquired the Summer Institute for the Gifted (SIG) offering summer camps for gifted and talented children aged between eleven and seventeen. In 2009 SIG became part of the National Society for the Gifted and Talented, a non-profit 501 (c) (3) US charity. This allowed it to maintain and build on its good standing at its prestigious campus locations such as Princeton and Yale. Led by Barbara Swicord, SIG is now the leading Gifted and Talented programme in the US for children aged 9-17.

AIFS has flourished over the years because it has always put the safety and welfare of its students first, as well as offering very high-quality programmes.

We seek to achieve Ken Blanchard's advice to persuade our students to give 'rave' reviews of their experiences with AIFS. We regularly ask our students what they think of their AIFS experience. In 2010, 95 per cent said they would recommend AIFS to a friend.

The Importance of Bringing People Together

There are nearly 7 billion people in our world today. Despite the vast increase in wealth in recent years, there are still many areas of the world which suffer from religious and cultural conflicts. Through AIFS I think we are playing an important if small part in creating international understanding. It is crucial that young people from different countries have the opportunity to learn about each other's cultures, languages and lifestyles by studying or working abroad. The mission of AIFS is even more important today than in was forty-eight years ago when AIFS was founded in Cincinnati, Ohio, in September 1964.

We have had many letters of support from our alumni. For example, Congressman Russ Carnahan, the former Democratic congressman representing Missouri's third district, who is a member of the House Foreign Affairs Committee, wrote

AIFS has a strong reputation of opening doors for students around the world, including myself. My time studying abroad in London at Richmond, The American International University in London, remains one of the most important foundations of my education. By getting to get know people and their way of life overseas as a college student I became better prepared to serve in Congress, where diplomatic engagement is as important as ever. But the truth is the experience can be valuable to all students. It is important that people have a better understanding of their neighbours around the world and the outstanding work of AIFS is making that a reality.

In the forty-eight years of its existence, AIFS has had many challenges to overcome including the effect on enrolment of international crises such as the Lockerbie bombing of Pan Am Flight 103 in December 1988, the Gulf Wars, the 9/11 terrorist attacks on New York and Pennsylvania, as well as the July 2005 terrorist attack on London. We employ 350 highly competent staff worldwide. Their competence and dedication is the prime reason for our success.

What of the future? After receiving wise advice from our professional advisers, including Stephen Rasch of Loeb Block in New York and Robert Maas, Chris Lintott and Clifford Joseph in London, I have made provision in my will to ensure that both Richmond and AIFS continue after I pass on. I thus hope that my life's work in creating AIFS will continue to flourish and help to bring the world together.

Although now in my seventies, I still remain actively involved in the work of AIFS. I was delighted in 2010 to be able to celebrate the enrollment of 1.5 million students in the various AIFS programmes since we launched in that small Cincinnati flat in 1964. Our new alumni programme will bring many of those students together. Over those five decades, I like to think we have done a lot to make the world a smaller place and helped to build a sense of understanding between young people from different countries. That is also an important goal of Richmond University.

7

AN AMERICAN UNIVERSITY IN LONDON

The Story of Richmond, the American International University in London and the Challenges of Setting up a New Private University in Britain

One of my proudest achievements was helping to found a new university in London. Richmond would become a pioneering liberal arts and private non-profit institution based on the American model of higher education. The new university grew out of the requirements of AIFS: we badly needed a London campus for our American study abroad students. Tony Lonsdale, who directed our college programmes, found the perfect place in an old divinity college on a wonderful 10-acre site at the top of Richmond Hill.

The original Wesleyan Theological College was founded by the Methodist Missionary Society in 1843 to train Methodist missionaries. A very distinguished architect, Andrew Trimen, designed the buildings using Bath stone to resemble an Oxbridge college. The missionary college flourished and at its peak had nearly 500 students. Many of the missionaries trained at Richmond brought back seeds and cuttings from such countries as Nepal and China to plant in the lovely gardens of the college. In 1870, Richmond became a constituent college of the University of London awarding divinity degrees. But 100 years later, enrolment at Richmond had fallen to just thirty male ordinands, as there was little demand by then to be trained as a Methodist Missionary. AIFS was ready to take up the empty beds, and nearly 100 AIFS students stayed there in 1970.

By this stage, with a second training college in Bristol, the Methodist Missionary Society and Church wanted to close Richmond. But we had a lease for our students and there were strict educational requirements linked to the site, so finding a buyer would not be easy. As President of AIFS, I met several times with Cyril Bennett, the director of the trust which owned the college. Cyril and I got on well, with my family background in missionary work providing a bond. Cyril agreed to sell half the site, including most of the buildings, to AIFS for £300,000 on the proviso that it be used for educational purposes, with the remaining five acres of land being sold to Richmond Council for the founding of a new primary school. As AIFS was still a small organisation and did not have £300,000 to purchase the site, Cyril generously granted us a mortgage which we paid off within ten years. A second campus was opened by Richmond in 1978 in Kensington in St Alban's Grove and Ansdell Street, for its third- and fourth-year students as well as the US study abroad students.

It was to prove a strong investment. Those early days of Richmond were focused on providing the study abroad programme for US students. But by the start of the eighties, the college's new president, William Petrek, decided Richmond should become an independent US liberal arts college awarding its own degrees. He obtained a licence to award US undergraduate degrees from the Washington DC Board of Education and formal accreditation from the Middle States Association of Colleges and Schools (now the Middle States Commission on Higher Education), which was granted in 1981. When Washington DC closed its education department, Richmond moved its accreditation to Delaware, which still licenses its degrees. Bill was an outstanding president who served for twelve years from 1980 to 1992. Under his tenure, Richmond developed a range of excellent undergraduate degree courses and recruited students from all over the world.

In March 1988, Richmond was honoured by a visit from Princess Diana to open our new classroom facilities in Young Street, off High Street Kensington, on the site of where the Spencer family – to which she belonged – had a London home. I briefed Diana on her visit and said how honoured we were by her presence. She replied modestly that she was only a twenty-seven-year-old girl and felt it was an honour to be invited. Naturally there was a huge press crowd outside the building. But Diana insisted on attending a class. So I took her into a Shakespeare class where our students were studying the sonnets. The professor read out Sonnet 18, 'Shall I compare thee to a summer's day?' The next day, the *Daily Mirror* front page was headlined, 'Shall I compare thee to a summer's Di?'

It was, of course, difficult establishing an independent university in England which had no government funding. However, the quality of its programmes attracted students from distinguished families all over the world, including the daughter of General Haig, the Commander of NATO Forces in Europe, the daughter of the King of Malaysia and members of the Indian Tata family. Indeed, because of the interest in its

Art History and Design course, Richmond opened branch campuses in Florence and Rome, which have become very popular, with a current enrolment of over 300 students.

Gaining proper accreditation in both the US and the UK is important for a private university. It provides students with reassurance about the quality of their degrees and ensures that the university itself meets exacting standards. In 1995, AIFS, which then still owned the college, decided its future would be better if it became an independent non-profit college, a decision strongly supported by the Middle States Commission. Richmond inaugurated its first postgraduate courses in 1998 with a Master of Business Administration degree. Richmond received approval from the UK Privy Council, which governs these matters, to change its name from a college to a university. The Privy Council has also recognised its right to award degrees since 1990. Richmond has also been accredited by the leading European distance learning provider, the Open University in the UK, since 1996. The OU validates all Richmond's undergraduate degrees, enabling its students resident in the UK and the European Union to apply for limited student grants. Uniquely, they receive both an American and a British degree.

The university has a bicameral structure consisting of a Board of Trustees and a Board of Academic Governors. The trustees are responsible for general policy, oversight of finances, appointment of senior staff and administration while the Academic Governors ensure that academic standards are maintained, as well as advising faculty on curriculum issues.

Richmond has succeeded not least because it has enjoyed some great leaders. Among the distinguished chairs and vice-chairs of governors have been the modern historian Lord (Asa) Briggs of Lewes, the art historian Sir Ernst Gombrich and the linguist Lord (Randolph) Quirk of Bloomsbury. The current chair, Peter Williams, continues to provide the university with invaluable support. All eight presidents have served the university with distinction, with Bill Petrek's vision in turning the college into a university a key turning point in its history.

Richmond has awarded honorary doctorates to many important figures since it became a university in 1990 including many with strong transatlantic connections. Among them were Sir Robin Renwick, the former British Ambassador in Washington, Lord (Richard) Attenborough of Richmond upon Thames, the late Garry Weston, Lord Harris of Peckham, Hon Phil Lader, former US Ambassador to the Court of St James, Graham Zellick, Michael Portillo, Sir Robert Worcester and George Weston (see Appendix 16).

But the very survival of the university was threatened when the UK government embarked on a major clampdown of students from outside the European Union in recent years. A new category of Highly Trusted Status was introduced, which has been given to most state-funded universities and further education colleges in the UK, enabling them to gain visas for their non-European students. Without this status, it would have been impossible for Richmond to survive. Achieving this status was an important success for the current president, Dr John Annette, who was previously the Pro Vice Master for Public Engagement and Professor of Citizenship Education at Birkbeck College, University of London. He was appointed in 2011 and since then has transformed the institution, adding new degree courses and greatly strengthening its staff and research profile. With Highly Trusted Status, students from across the globe come to study at Richmond. The university now enrols 1,000 full-time students from more than 100 countries with 750 students in London and 250 in Italy.

The Richmond campus is now used for freshmen and sophomores while the Kensington campus is for juniors and seniors, visiting American students and postgraduate students. There is the potential to grow to 1,500 students across both campuses, and the university also arranges study abroad programmes at its own campuses in Florence and Rome. It is particularly encouraging that so many students rate their time at Richmond so highly, with 97 per cent of American students rating their experience as excellent or good in 2011.

Relations with China

China has now become a global superpower to match the United States. Its economic might is growing each year, and its importance to the world with it. I have always felt it was vital to engage with China, well before its current pre-eminent status. The Specialist Schools Trust, which I founded, developed a strong reputation for promoting Mandarin teaching in English schools and providing English support for the advancement of Chinese education. Of course, these days, with Shanghai rated as best in the world for maths in the PISA rankings published by the OECD, we have plenty to learn from the Chinese about education too.

Richmond's relations with China go back to 1979, a year after Deng Xiaoping, the great reforming leader who introduced a market economy to the People's Republic, took office. In 1979, I joined a delegation from Richmond to sign an exchange agreement with the then Beijing Language and Cultural Institute. It was quite remarkable visiting the city with Walter McCann, who was then president at Richmond, just as it was opening up to the wider world and I have seen huge changes since as China has become an economic superpower. I had my first visit to Tiananmen Square and the Forbidden City, the great imperial palace that housed Chinese emperors for five centuries.

Under our agreement – one of the first to be agreed by the new regime – Beijing sent teachers to Richmond who had not had the opportunity to complete their Chinese degrees because of the Cultural Revolution which had forced them to work on farms rather than in the classroom. In return, the institute accepted a large number of our American students who spent a summer or a semester in Beijing. Before Deng, such exchanges would have been unthinkable. Once the deal had been signed, I gained new insights into Chinese attitudes to hospitality. I invited our new partners at the institute to lunch to celebrate the deal. But they felt that they should have invited us to eat. So, after having had a huge lunch, they invited us to be their guests for a banquet that evening. We were certainly well-fed that day. Ten teachers initially came to Richmond for a year and received a Richmond degree as they were given credit for their previous study in China. The programme lasted a decade, but had to be suspended after the events of 1989 in Tiananmen Square, though at the time our students were hired by Western media as translators, placing themselves in danger in the process.

However, a new agreement between Richmond and the Beijing Language and Culture University has been signed more recently. And in 2006 and 2007 through the support of Madame Yang Meng, the Deputy Secretary General of the China Education Association for International Exchange, Richmond bid for and received a £1 million contract with Gordon Brown's help from the British government to arrange six-month internships for 100 Chinese students. Uniquely, as an American university operating in the United Kingdom, Richmond received formal approval from the Chinese government as a recognised British university. The university is planning to establish a Confucius Institute to teach Mandarin and to encourage Chinese students to apply for enrolment.

I have had three further visits to China since we first negotiated that historic deal, and have noticed a lot of changes. Where Beijing was then a city of bicycles it is today choking in the fumes of cars and motorbikes. The cities are unrecognisable in their scale of development and the standard of living has undoubtedly improved for many people. But since Tiananmen Square, China also feels less free in some respects than it did in those heady days. Nevertheless, I am convinced that the links we build with China through such exchanges will be of huge value in the years ahead to all our countries.

The Future

Under Dr Annette's dynamic leadership, a five-year development plan has been prepared by Richmond and approved by the Middle States Commission. Richmond has applied to the Qualifications and Assessment Authority (QAA) in the United Kingdom to award its own British degrees, rather than having them accredited by the Open University, while retaining the right to award American degrees. David Willetts, the higher education minister, has lowered the minimum enrolment for a private US degree-awarding university from 4,000 to 1,000, and the university has the space to double its student numbers in London, which would ensure that it could do even more to further international relations. Richmond also plans to broaden its undergraduate and graduate degrees and to establish its research profile.

Richmond's success has largely been based on applying successful US higher education initiatives to a university in England. Students benefit from a broadly based initial curriculum for first and second year. They can gain credits for their work which they can use at other universities, or they can bring credits from other universities to Richmond. There are broadly based admission criteria including A-levels, International Baccalaureate, US Scholastic Aptitude Tests (SATs) and Advanced Placement test scores. And students can pick from a wide choice of courses for their major in years three and four.[6]

With increased tuition fees in England, there has been a lot of discussion about creating more private universities. Doing so could provide healthy competition to existing state-funded providers, more choice for students and more efficient use of UK taxpayers' money. A big advantage of private universities like Richmond, as well as the University of Buckingham and Regents College, is that they are not subject to the micro-management of the government and its agencies. They also have a culture of actively seeking the support of private sponsors and business as well as their alumni, which is still a lot more common in the US than in the UK, despite recent government match funding to stimulate the development of endowments in higher education.

I have been proud of my association with Richmond since its inception. What started out as a convenient way to accommodate our exchange students has blossomed into a distinguished and growing university in its own right. The philosophy of Richmond is the same at that which inspired us to establish AIFS in 1964, and which I hope continues to inspire its thousands of alumni across the world.

8

POLITICAL ANIMAL

Standing for Parliament, Serving on the Greater London Council & Ideas for Cutting Waste in Government

Because of my entrepreneurial background I have always thought of myself as a Tory. There was entrepreneurial as well as missionary zeal in the Taylor blood, from my great-grandfather's successful Pimlico business to my uncle's bathroom supplies business in Yorkshire. So I always felt drawn to the Conservatives, which I felt were more supportive of the needs of businesspeople. At Cambridge, I chaired my college's Conservative Association and I used to speak in the Cambridge Union debating society. Harvard Business School reinforced my entrepreneurial instincts. So it seemed natural when I returned to England In April 1970 to join the Kensington Conservatives Association. Over the next few years I would try – and fail – to become a Member of Parliament, and would play a small but significant role in London politics.

I was soon elected deputy chairman of the new combined Kensington and Chelsea constituency on the recommendation of the then chairman, George Pole. But I had also got politics in my blood by this stage, and I felt that I could offer more at a national level. So, I went to Conservative Central Office before the 1970 General Election to offer my services. In that election, the pundits all expected the Labour Prime Minister Harold Wilson to win another term, and they were backed to some extent by the opinion polls. I was asked to help a Conservative candidate, Spencer Le Marchant, an extremely tall old Etonian, win a Labour-held marginal High Peak seat in Derbyshire.

In High Peak, I learned a lot about running a political campaign, as I helped to arrange the candidate's speaking engagements around the local villages and towns, and knocked on doors to get out the Tory vote. Nationally, the pundits and the pollsters were wrong: it was the Conservatives' Edward Heath rather than Harold Wilson who won the election, and he did so because his party was successful in marginal constituencies like High Peak. Le Marchant turned Peter Jackson's Labour majority of 814 in the 1966 election into a 1504 Conservative majority, with a swing of around 4 per cent that matched the national mood.

I was pleased to see the Conservatives back in power. But High Peak was also an eye-opener for me as it taught me the basics of running a successful election campaign. I hoped that the lessons I had learned in Derbyshire would help me to win a seat myself when I applied and was approved to be on the official Conservative Party candidates' list. Meanwhile, I continued to serve as the deputy chair of the Kensington Association.

My chance to stand moved a step closer in the autumn of 1973 when a vacancy emerged for a candidate in the Labour-held seat of Huddersfield East. Having been born to Yorkshire parents – my mother's name, after all, was Hebden – and having spent so much of my peripatetic childhood in that great county, I felt like I was coming home. Huddersfield East was never going to be an easy prospect. The local Labour MP was a Second World War naval veteran called Joseph Mallalieu who had occupied the seat and its predecessor since the Labour landslide of 1945. His daughter, Ann, would become both a Labour peer and a keen advocate of the Countryside Alliance. However, Mallalieu's majority had been slashed from 10,789 to 4,997 at the previous election and it was not a hopeless cause.

My Yorkshire roots obviously impressed the local association, and I was selected as the party's candidate. We bought a house in Almondbury, and Judy and I spent a considerable amount of time getting ourselves known in the area. However, it was not a good time to be fighting in the Conservative cause. Ted Heath was increasingly unpopular, as he was held to ransom by the unions. This was the time of power cuts and television shutting down after *News at Ten*. I fought a good campaign in February 1974, using the slogan borrowed from a popular song, 'Nice One Cyril'. But with Harold Wilson back in No. 10, Labour regained some of the votes it had lost in 1970 and I lost by 7,304 votes.

Nevertheless, this was seen as a creditable campaign by Central Office, and they were keen to keep me as a candidate. Meanwhile I had resumed my AIFS activities full-time and had returned to Kenya for the first time since my days on National Service to set up an exchange programme at Oloitokitok Outward Bound School on the slopes of Mount Kilimanjaro. Harold Wilson may have won the 1974 election, but he had not got a working majority in parliament. So he called another election for October. I received an urgent message while I was at the Kenyan school from the Yorkshire Conservative Party inviting me to stand for the marginal seat of Keighley. Joan Hall had lost the seat in the February election to Labour's Bob Cryer by fewer than 1,000 votes, and it was the thirty-fifth-most marginal seat in the country at the time. I flew home to meet the local association.

The Keighley constituency is almost evenly split in its population between the largely Labour-voting Keighley town and the Conservative spa town of Ilkley, as well as the rural areas of Craven and Worth Valley which have strong Conservative votes. It is a classic marginal. At the selection meeting there was a large audience which included the then Chair of the Keighley Young Conservatives, Eric Pickles – who now serves as Secretary of State for Communities and Local Government. They asked what role Judy would play in the campaign, as she was American. I suggested she replied to that question directly but that was overruled. So I then pointed out that Winston Churchill had an American mother and I felt it was an advantage having an American wife. That seemed to satisfy them. I became the Conservative candidate for Keighley.

Although I campaigned hard in the few months before the election, the national swing was running in Wilson's favour, and I was defeated by 3,000 out of some 43,000 votes. This was still regarded by the local association as a very good result and they wanted me to stay on as the candidate for the next election which, as it happened, would not take place until 1979. They assured me I would win the seat at the next election.

I thought long and hard, but the truth was that what I really wanted was a safe Conservative seat, and preferably closer to the capital. At that stage in my career and with a daughter who was not yet five years of age, the thought of travelling to Keighley every weekend for five years to fight a Labour-held seat was not appealing. So I resigned the candidature. Not surprisingly this was not well-regarded either locally or at Conservative Cabinet Office. Because I had resigned as the candidate for a marginal seat, there was little chance of me being adopted for a safe seat, although I was short-listed for several and came close to selection in Bournemouth and Crawley. In the General Election of 1979, during Margaret Thatcher's landslide, Bob Cryer clung onto Keighley by just eighty votes. But from 1983 to 1992 the seat was held by the Conservative Gary Waller. Locals said that if I had remained as their candidate, I could have won the seat in 1979. To this day, I wonder would my life have been different had I become an MP. Even more importantly, could I have held the seat in either 1992 or 1997?

London Politics

Somewhat chastened by my attempt to get to Westminster, I started to look at alternative ways to enter public service which might prove easier to combine with family life and my work with AIFS. In 1977 I was given the opportunity to stand as the Greater London Council (GLC) Conservative candidate for Ruislip-Northwood, a comparatively safe seat in the Borough of Hillingdon. I campaigned hard against an unpopular Labour Leader of the Hillingdon Council, Alderman John Bartlett. This was a year when the Conservatives won a landslide on the GLC, as the Labour government under James Callaghan was in the midst of a huge economic crisis. But local politics played a big part too: Bartlett was being accused of wanting to build council houses in people's gardens, which was at the heart of his unpopularity. The Conservatives took thirty-two seats from Labour across the GLC, and I won the GLC seat with 23,058 votes, a majority of 18,599 over my Labour opponent, P. J. Goody. It was the largest majority in London, and represented a swing of 20 per cent. I was delighted with the scale of the result and pleased to be part of a winning team at County Hall.

For the next nine years until Margaret Thatcher abolished the Greater London Council (GLC) in 1986, I served as the member of the GLC for Ruislip-Northwood. The Conservative leader, Sir Horace Cutler, appointed me to be chairman of the council's Professional and General Services Committee, which supervised the employment of the 25,000 GLC staff. The GLC had a reputation for profligacy which was resented by London ratepayers, particularly in the outer suburbs like those I represented. There were simply too many people employed at County Hall and across the capital, and with the economy facing serious problems nationally, it was vital to cut costs. In four years, I was able to reduce the number of GLC staff by almost half. Together with George Tremlett, who was the GLC's head of housing policy and someone who had radical views on how to improve social housing, I also helped persuade Horace Cutler either to sell the 200,000 GLC council homes to their tenants, or transfer them to the boroughs.

Getting Better Value from Public Spending

This was a time when I came to realise how much money is wasted in the public sector, and how much can be done to gain greater efficiency without harming the quality of services. I wrote a policy paper on reducing public expenditure during my days on the GLC called *The Elected Member's Guide to Reducing Public Expenditure* which Margaret Thatcher said she found very useful.

Today, when the coalition of Conservatives and Liberal Democrats is trying to impose cuts in public expenditure to reduce the deficit that they inherited, it is timely to consider how best to cut costs. Within its first 100 days, the coalition produced a radical set of proposals to solve Britain's problems. The coalition inherited one of the worst economies in the Western world, with a massive budget deficit of 11 per cent of GDP, higher than Spain or Italy, or even Greece, and a national unemployment rate of 10 per cent.

The new government resolved to reduce the budget deficit essentially by spending cuts, though they have also increased value added tax. Most government departments are being reduced by one quarter, and there are radical plans to reduce dependency on welfare and to make work pay. This is crucial. In some areas of Britain, such as the North East area surrounding Newcastle, because of the disappearance of the coal, shipbuilding and steel industries, almost two thirds of the working population work for the state or local government or are on welfare.

However, I know how difficult it is to reduce public expenditure with strong opposition from both the public and trade unions. When it came to halving the GLC's staff, Horace Cutler told us to ask four questions about each of the functions which the Greater London Council performed at that time. First, was the function necessary at all? Too often in government, initiative is piled upon initiative, or programmes are retained long after they have served their original purpose. A lot can be done by looking again at everything a council or government department is doing, and eliminating those things that no longer serve any useful purpose. The present government has got rid of many regional tiers of governance, for example, and has abolished the primary care trusts in the health service to devolve power to general practitioners. When the Conservatives took control in 1977, there were 130 GLC committees employing hundreds of council staff to produce the paper necessary to service them. A day after our landslide, Sir Horace Cutler cut these committees down to just twenty-seven with commensurate savings in staff numbers. Officers reported that the council's business proceeded much more smoothly with fewer committees.

At the GLC, we determined that, as London's population had fallen by 1 million in the previous decades, there was a gross surplus of approximately 50,000 homes over households desiring homes in the Greater London area. The big housing problem in the capital at that time was not insufficient homes, but the number of sub-standard homes which needed renovation. So, George Tremlett rapidly cut the number of new homes being built by the GLC from 6,000 to fewer than 1,000 a year. He used the money saved to spend more on modernising the council's existing stock. This step alone allowed us to reduce the GLC staff by 10 per cent, or 3,000 people, through cuts in the Housing Department, alongside parallel cuts in the Valuer's Department, which had been employing hundreds of people finding new housing sites, and in the Architect's Department, which had employed many architects and quantity surveyors on the construction of new houses. Too many questionable local authority functions are still required by statute, and these statutes need to be repealed if really effective progress is to be made. There are also unnecessary European Union rules on health and safety and employment which cost huge sums of money.

Sir Horace's second question was, if the function was necessary, should it be done by the GLC, or could it be done more effectively by the private sector or even another authority such as a London borough? Here, too, we found real savings. By 1977, the GLC was employing 1,000 people in its own direct labour construction branch. This department was building houses at a cost far higher than private contractors. By closing the branch – and putting the work that still needed to be done out to tender – we were able to save the ratepayers millions of pounds each year. Again in the field of housing, the GLC, through lack of clarity in the London Government Act of 1963 and for political reasons, had duplicated the boroughs' housing management function by creating its own vast housing bureaucracy of over 7,000 staff to look after the GLC's 200,000 council houses and flats. Here we were to be pioneers in one of the great social changes of the Thatcher years. The sale of council houses to their tenants was a great way to encourage people to take more pride in their homes and to encourage a sense of responsibility and independence. It was to prove one of Mrs Thatcher's most popular policies, and one of her more enduring legacies. A large number of these GLC houses and flats were sold to their tenants. George then persuaded all except a handful of London's boroughs to take over the running of the remaining GLC's houses in their areas. The result was better management of the housing stock – and many proud new owners – with lower costs to the ratepayers in areas like Ruislip who had footed the bill for all the needless bureaucracy.

Cutler's third question was to ask whether we needed to do quite so many of those functions that we had determined should continue to be done by the GLC, while his fourth question asked how to ensure that the function, if necessary, was being performed efficiently. These were important questions, but also harder to answer than his first two. In these areas, both the late Leslie Chapman and Sir Derek Rayner had done important work. Chapman's *Your Disobedient Servant* should be required reading for any council establishment or government office.[7] His principal tool to determine if a function was being run efficiently was the use of a three-man efficiency team. This method proved very successful in the seventies in reducing waste in the old Ministry of Works.

Chapman recommended that the three-man teams should include a member with audit or accounting experience, someone from outside the council's or government's service to give a private sector view and someone with expertise in the subject matter from within the department being examined. The teams were given sixty working days to complete their reports. Care was taken to maintain good relations with both unions and department heads. Indeed, Chapman believed that the team must persuade the supervisor of a department and the unions of the wisdom of any reforms recommended. Without this concurrence, little or no progress would be made.[8]

It is important that governments realise that they don't always need to reinvent the wheel to make a difference. I did send David Cameron a copy of the booklet, though, and hope it will be useful in his goal to reduce wasteful public expenditure.

Cameron also sought to promote a new political philosophy which he called the 'Big Society' where he called for more of Britain's public services to be run by the private or charitable sector such as having the power to run or create new schools. New free schools are being introduced in response to parental demand rather than the planning needs of local authorities.

Why has Britain suddenly become so audacious in resolving its problems? One reason, I am convinced, is the Thatcherite legacy, but the principal reason is strong leadership, with the two coalition parties willing to demand and require that radical action be taken to eliminate the financial deficit.

Throughout the rich world, including the United States, government has simply got too big. The Cameron government is showing how the problem can be solved. At present, unlike in the 1980s, there is no Reaganesque echo on the US side of the Atlantic to the Thatcher reforms. Despite the Tea Party zeal, the Republicans do not appear to have a coherent strategy to reduce the US government deficit which is now 9 per cent of GNP. President Obama has not yet produced a viable plan to bring back prosperity and the entrepreneurial spirit to the United States. After his victory in 2012, President Obama will need a credible plan and good advisers to get to grips with the burgeoning deficit, and they will need bipartisan support in doing so from Congress.

The Abolition of the GLC

I enjoyed my service in the GLC greatly. When the Conservatives lost power in 1981 to Ken Livingstone, I was appointed as the opposition spokesman on transport, something which was highly controversial under Livingstone, who sought to fund fare reductions from the rates. I was then elected deputy leader of the Conservative Group in the GLC in 1984 when Alan Greengross took over from Richard Brew as the Conservative leader, who had earlier succeeded Sir Horace Cutler as leader.

Alan and I enjoyed making life a misery for Livingstone, whose outrageous antics prompted Margaret Thatcher to abolish the GLC. She particularly objected to Livingstone using the roof of County Hall, which faced the Houses of Parliament on the other side of the River Thames, to highlight the growing number of the unemployed in London. But Livingstone also attracted popular opprobrium for his support for minority causes and his hosting of Sinn Féin leaders in London at a time when the IRA campaign was at its most brutal. Of course, abolition was not the end of Livingstone's career. He would return as elected Mayor of London in 2000, a post he would hold for eight years until he was defeated by Boris Johnson, for the Conservatives, in 2008. He failed to gain re-election in 2012.

I was not, however, a supporter of wholesale abolition of the GLC. It certainly needed reform: we had shown that with the savings we had been able to make, particularly in the field of housing. There was also plenty of scope to devolve functions to the thirty-two boroughs and reduce the burden on ratepayers in the capital. But, a great city like London needs a citywide authority to supervise such crucial issues as transport, road maintenance, strategic planning and rate equalisation. I wrote a popular Bow Group paper, *London Preserved*, which put these arguments forcibly.

My argument was that all the Prime Minister had to do was to wait until the 1985 GLC election, when the Conservatives would have undoubtedly taken back control from Livingstone. This did not go down well with the Iron Lady, who I had first got to know informally during the 1970s through my work at the Centre for Policy Studies. The CPS had declined to publish my paper, which was published by the Bow Group, but it was at a CPS dinner at No. 10 that she called me a 'wet' for writing this paper. The term 'wet' was one of the strongest forms of abuse for a Conservative at the time: those in the cabinet who were seen as 'wet' were regarded as not being true believers in the Thatcherite cause. Yet I was a believer in the need for much greater efficiency and savings in the public sector. I had shown that through my actions at the GLC. John Redwood, then Mrs Thatcher's chief policy adviser, told me that I was endangering my political career by publishing the paper, even though he said he thought it was a good paper. Norman Tebbit, when he was party chairman, told me my paper had done a lot of harm to the Conservative Party in the House of Commons and had reduced the government majority.

However, I still feel that I was right to make the argument that I did, and the abolition of the GLC arguably helped turn Livingstone from an extremist pariah into a popular victim. I have no doubt it was that victimhood that survived in the popular memory and helped him to win election as mayor when Tony Blair, as Labour Prime Minister, reintroduced London government in 2000. The elected mayor and Greater London Assembly is likely to be a sustainable model for the capital, and proved crucial in winning the Olympic Games. Indeed, David Cameron has tried to promote the elected mayor model to other cities, though the only big English cities outside the capital to adopt the idea so far are Liverpool and Bristol.

Despite considerable support for my views on the GLC in the Conservative Party, including among Conservative MPs, the GLC was abolished in 1986, having secured a narrow majority in parliament. The Inner London Education Authority would go soon after. While agencies were left in charge of some strategic functions, most matters were delegated to the boroughs. It didn't take long for the campaign for strategic government in the capital to reassert itself and to win eventually the cross-party consensus it has today.

But the abolition of the GLC had further significance for me. From 1986, I was no longer a Conservative councillor and seemed unlikely to have any future political career – would I always just be a 'nearly' man? However, I would find other ways to provide public service over the next two decades, and would do so together with successive governments.

9
SPECIALIST SCHOOLS & ACADEMIES

The Story of the City Technology Colleges (CTCs) & Specialist Schools & Academies Trust

By 1986, the GLC had been abolished and I was no longer a Conservative councillor. I felt stung by the criticism I had received for my arguments against wholesale abolition, and was sure that my days of political influence were over. But Margaret Thatcher had other ideas. Youth unemployment had grown substantially as the economy was restructured in the early 1980s and was a major political concern. There were over 1 million young people out of work by this time, and worries about their futures were as strong then as they became in 2011 when the figure again reached such levels.

By this stage, despite their refusal to publish my paper opposing abolition, I was still a director of her favourite think tank, the Centre for Policy Studies, which she had founded with Sir Keith Joseph in 1974 to champion the cause of economic liberalism. She asked me to organise an all-day CPS conference at the House of Lords which would be chaired by Lord Young of Graffham, then the Employment Secretary, to discuss the issue.

I invited twenty of the country's leading industrialists to the all-day conference, which she attended herself. The industrial leaders were unanimous in their advice to the Prime Minister. They told her that young people could not find jobs because the schools were not teaching their pupils the right skills and they recommended that the government use private sector support to set up and directly fund 100 technology colleges.

Thus was born an idea which would make a big contribution to school improvement for the next twenty-five years. At this stage, the plan was to introduce City Technology Colleges, independent schools backed by state and industry funding that would provide a free education to children in urban areas focused on modern technology. The reforming Education Secretary Kenneth Baker would announce the idea at the Conservative Party Conference in Bournemouth that October.

I had got to know Kenneth Baker in his previous appointment as Local Government Minister. Although Margaret Thatcher did not like my Bow Group paper *London Preserved*, Ken believed the paper contained some good sense. And following my paper for the CPS, *The Right Approach to More Jobs*, he decided I was the right man to lead the CTC initiative. Ken's 1988 Education Reform Act was probably the single most important piece of legislation on schools since the Second World War. It introduced the national curriculum and the key stages of a child's education that allowed regular testing. It gave headteachers control over most of their own budgets. It allowed schools to opt for greater control of their land, staffing and admissions as grant-maintained schools. And it paved the way for CTCs. Ken is also indefatigable – he has more recently had a new lease of life promoting university technical colleges to provide an industry-focused education for fourteen- to sixteen-year-olds. He gave me tremendous support at this time and it was a pleasure to work for him.

Despite our earlier disagreements, Mrs Thatcher approved my appointment as Baker's special adviser to organise the project. As is usual, I had to sign the Official Secrets Act requiring me to safeguard confidential government information. Special advisers, who are usually political appointees with some expertise in the departmental brief, have been the subject of controversy more recently, but they are a vital part of getting things done in Whitehall.

On my first day in my new job at the Department of Education and Science, I was shown my office, which was a small room in a remote part of the department which then was situated on top of Waterloo Station, across the road from County Hall. I was allocated no support staff, so I persuaded Kenneth to let me work out of my own AIFS office in 37 Queen's Gate where I had excellent back-up. On my first day at the department, I was given a box of cheques by John Hedger, who was the senior official in charge of the new initiative. The cheques were from potential private sector donors. But the education department had no experience of handling private donations, so novel was the idea of such sponsorship, and he did not know what to do with them. It was clear that we would need to establish a new charity. Thus was born the City Technology Colleges Trust in May 1987.

The inaugural meeting of the new trust was held at the Berkeley Hotel in 1987 with the original group of sponsors including Gordon White of the Hanson Trust, Stanley Kalms of Dixons, Philip Harris of Carpetright, Harry Djanogly, Randolph Quirk, the vice-chancellor of London University; Heather Brigstock, the headmistress of St Paul's Girls' School; Ronald Halstead of British Steel, Peter Vardy, of the Reg Vardy Group; Garry Weston, chairman of Associated British Foods, Geoffrey Leigh and Michael Wakeford, clerk of the Mercers.

Tony Lonsdale was appointed as the first chief executive, and we established a small CTC Trust office in Young Street, Kensington where he was based. There was good initial support for the new initiative, and £44 million of sponsorship was raised between 1987 and 1993. I was honoured when Lord Baker recommended that I be appointed a Knight Bachelor in the 1989 Birthday Honours for services to education in recognition of the success of the CTC initiative. But the CTC model, where industry would contribute up to £2 million towards the capital cost of the new schools with the government paying the teaching costs, required too great a commitment for many potential sponsors.

CTCs were non-selective: many used a form of fair banding to ensure that they had an intake across the ability range. They also reflected wider moves to provide state schools with greater freedom as a result of Kenneth Baker's legislation. As headteachers were given a larger proportion of their school budgets, they no longer had to seek the permission of local authorities for how they spent it. It was also a time when schools were being encouraged to 'opt out' of local authority control and be funded directly by Whitehall with control over staffing, admissions and land as 'grant-maintained schools'. The CTCs had similar freedoms to the GM schools but had a strong specialist focus on technology, although they taught a broad curriculum. They were, however, not required to teach the new national curriculum that was being introduced in other state-funded schools.

The fifteen CTCs established from 1988 to 1993 were:

City Technology College	Major Sponsors
Kingshurst CTC in Birmingham (1988)	Hanson Trust and Lucas Aerospace
Djanogly CTC in Nottingham (1989)	Sir Harry Djanogly
Macmillan CTC in Middlesbrough (1989)	BAT Industries, Sir John Hall
Dixons CTC in Bradford (1990)	Dixons, Haking Wong Enterprises
Leigh CTC in Dartford (1990)	Sir Geoffrey Leigh, Wellcome Trust
Thomas Telford CTC in Telford (1990)	The Worshipful Company of Mercers, Tarmac
Harris CTC in Croydon (1990)	Philip and Pauline Harris Charitable Trust
Emmanuel CTC in Gateshead (1990)	Reg Vardy, Safeway, Laings
Bacon's CTC in Southwark (1991)	Church of England, Philip and Pauline Harris Charitable Trust, London Docklands Corporation
Brooke Weston in Corby (1991)	Hugh de Capell Brooke and Garry Weston of Associated British Foods and the Weston Foundation
BRIT School in Selhurst, Croydon (1991)	BRIT Trust, Donations from six major recording companies and proceeds from the Knebworth Concert in 1990 organised by Sir Richard Branson
Haberdashers' CTC in Lewisham (1991)	The Worshipful Company of Haberdashers
ADT College in Wandsworth (now Ashcroft Technology Academy) (1991)	ADT and Lord Ashworth
Landau Forte CTC in Derby (1992)	Landau Foundation, Forte plc
John Cabot CTC in Bristol (1993)	Cable & Wireless, Wolfson Foundation

Source Material: 'City Technology Colleges – Conception and Legacy' by Christine Walter published by the SSAT 2007

The last CTC, John Cabot, was established in Bristol in 1993, backed by Cable & Wireless and the Wolfson Foundation. Today the original fifteen CTCs, most of which have since converted to academy status, are among the very best state schools in the country as shown in the chart below.

CTC	% 5+ A*-C grades including English and maths in 2011	% Eligible for free school meals
ADT, Wandsworth (Ashcroft Technology Academy)	71	27.8
Bacon's,Rotherhithe	66	45.9
BRIT, Croydon	68	10.5
Brooke Weston, Corby	84	7.2
Dixons*, Bradford	80	12.4
Djanogly**Nottingham	38	36.3
Emmanuel, Gateshead	88	7.3
Haberdashers,' Lewisham	78	24.1
Harris, Crystal Palace	95	11.6
John Cabot, Bristol	73	7.5
Kingshurst, Solihull	61	20.2
Landau Forte, Derby	64	13.5
Leigh*, Dartford	56	8.7
Macmillan*, Middlesbrough	66	26.2
Thomas Telford, Telford	98	10.0
AVERAGE	**72.4%**	17.9

* These schools are in the top 50 in the country in terms of contextual value added. The BRIT is 16th, Macmillan is 37th, Dixons 45th and Leigh 48th

** includes pupils from Forest Comprehensive School with which Djanogly merged in 2003 when it became an academy
Source: DFE Performance Tables

The freedom of CTCs meant that they were controversial with many local authorities and teaching unions, who saw them as a threat to their power. Some local schools also worried about the increased competition. But their biggest problem was their cost, and this meant that by 1992, when the economy slumped, there were just fifteen CTCs already committed or open. A less expensive alternative was needed.

I suggested an alternative, less expensive option – which would involve converting existing comprehensive schools to technology colleges. There would still be sponsorship: schools would be expected to raise £100,000 from industry, and would receive match funding from the government for capital costs, as well as additional per-pupil funding each year. In return, they needed to show how they would raise standards using their new technology specialism, and they would be expected to demonstrate progress after four years if they were to have the extra funding renewed. These were the first specialist schools.

Technology colleges, which would focus on design and technology, mathematics and science, while teaching the full National Curriculum, as was the case with all later specialist schools, were strongly supported by John Major, who had succeeded Margaret Thatcher as Prime Minister in 1990. I remained special adviser on the initiative with Kenneth's four Conservative successors, John McGregor, Kenneth Clarke, John Patten and Gillian Shephard. Gillian was Education Secretary from 1994 until 1997, and was particularly keen on specialist schools.

She arranged for a meeting with the Prime Minister, in the Cabinet Room at Downing Street in 1996. At that stage the initiative was limited to technology colleges, and had grown from fifty schools in 1993 to 245 schools. It was also limited to grant-maintained and faith-based voluntary-aided secondary schools. Gillian wanted to see all secondary schools becoming specialist, though when she initially talked of 'all schools', John Major thought she meant the 18,000 primaries as well as 3,200 secondary schools. I pointed out that it would cost comparatively little to convert all the secondary schools. Sponsors would contribute £100,000 of sponsorship to be matched by the government to pay for the necessary capital investment. In addition, successful schools applying for specialist status would be paid about £100,000 a year or £100 per pupil in addition to their regular funding. Thus 500 additional specialist schools would cost the government £50 million of capital investment plus an additional £25 million a year. John Major gave his support to increasing the number of specialist schools in view of their success. The programme would also expand to include specialisms in languages, sport and the arts. We owe Gillian Shephard a great deal.[9] But the Conservatives had been in power for seventeen years in 1996 and the political tide had started to turn. John Major had unexpectedly been re-elected in 1992 when he was challenged by Neil Kinnock for Labour. Since then, Labour had re-branded itself under a new leader, Tony Blair, who was riding high in the opinion polls. I realised that it was unlikely that the Conservatives would return to power at the General Election of 1997. If specialist schools were to continue, I therefore needed to gain the support of the Labour Party.

As it happened, as part of the Blairite changes, Labour had embarked on a radical overhaul of its education policy. David Blunkett had been appointed Shadow Education Secretary after Blair's election as Labour leader in 1994 and had embraced key Conservative reforms including the National Curriculum, regular testing and league tables. He had placed new emphasis on raising standards, particularly in literacy. And he had also started to speak in favour of greater diversity in schools and had not ruled out continuing with specialist schools. By several strokes of luck, I was able to convince Labour Party leaders of the effectiveness in raising standards of specialist schools. A key figure in this was Conor Ryan, who was David's key adviser on schools. We would write a book together eight years later.

David Blunkett, who would become Education and Employment Secretary from 1997 to 2001, was a remarkable figure. His ability to cope with all the demands of being a Secretary of State despite his being blind was an example to all those with a disability. He told me that when he attended a special boarding school for the blind, his teachers told him he should learn how to be a piano tuner, since it was unlikely he would get any other job. David studied for A-levels at the Royal National College for the Blind in Shrewsbury, studied at the Universities of Sheffield and Chester and then became a Sheffield city councillor, eventually becoming Leader of the Council before being elected to parliament in 1987 for the Sheffield constituency of Brightside. His working-class roots made him an important figure in Blair's Labour Party, as he understood both the party's roots and the need for reform.

I first got to know David thanks to a happy coincidence. David's son Hugh was at that time attending Yewlands Technology College in Sheffield, one of the earliest technology colleges. During a visit to the school in 1996 we had a long chat, from which a surprisingly warm friendship developed. When I offered him my help if and when he became Education Secretary, he got up and hugged me. At the same time, one of Labour's two spokesmen on schools in David's team was Estelle Morris, who by chance had been a teacher at Sydney Stringer Specialist Technology College in Coventry, and she also supported the concept of specialist schools. Labour's schools policy statement to the 1996 party conference included clear support for specialist schools provided that the programme was open to all maintained schools.

Although specialist schools had been accepted at this stage by Labour, I was keen to ensure that the programme would expand. Labour was not yet promising to spend any extra money on the public services. So, in December 1996, Tony Blair was invited to officially open the Carmel Specialist Technology College in Darlington, close to his own constituency. I was invited to accompany him on the train journey from London to Darlington and was given an hour to describe the specialist schools programme to the Labour leader and his adviser, Tim Allen. At the time there were only 200 specialist schools. Blair asked a lot of searching questions on such issues as the success of specialist schools and raising standards, admissions, community action and the role of sponsors. The future Prime Minister was greatly impressed by his visit to the Carmel Technology College. And the rest is history.

During the April 1997 General Election, the Labour and Conservative parties competed on the numbers of specialist schools they would establish if elected. David Blunkett said he wanted 1,000 specialist schools. Labour won a substantial majority at the General Election.

In May 1997, I was reappointed as a special adviser by David Blunkett to advise on specialist schools, the only Conservative adviser to keep my job. And though I subsequently resigned my membership of the Conservative Party, I did not join the Labour Party, as I remained committed to the ideas that I had argued for during the seventies and eighties. As his adviser, I wrote David a briefing note in Braille, outlining the problems he would face. The then Permanent Secretary, Michael Bichard, was very upset; firstly that I had retained my job as a special adviser and secondly that I had written David a confidential letter in Braille which the officials could not understand. Whitehall officials pride themselves on knowing everything that is being said or done where ministers are concerned, and I had found a way that circumvented official procedures. David was quite happy to receive advice in this way, but for the sake of good relations with his officials, I agreed to send the Permanent Secretary a printed version of my letter.

Under David Blunkett, with Estelle Morris as the schools minister, the specialist school programme grew rapidly, from 245 in 1997 to 700 by 2001. New specialisms were added and the programme was integrated with other key reform initiatives. Some changes were made to make it easier for schools: the sponsorship requirement was reduced to £50,000 from business, and schools were expected to use some of the extra money they received each year to work with other local schools. But in essence it remained as I had envisaged it in 1992. In 2000, Blunkett and Blair announced that Labour, if elected for a second term, would introduce City Academies, a new school designed to lift standards in deprived areas that was modelled on the City Technology College.

I was fortunate to develop a close friendly relationship with David. It was truly a privilege to work for him for four years developing the specialist schools and the academies initiative. After the 2001 election, David was promoted to Home Secretary and he served with distinction in that post until he resigned in 2004 after he had been accused of trying to speed up a visa for his friend's nanny. Although an investigation found no evidence to substantiate the charges, he resigned as he felt that questions over his honesty were damaging his government. I felt it was a real shame that such an issue could bring down such an able politician.

David was succeeded as Education Secretary by Estelle Morris, who had been his deputy in the previous parliament. Estelle had been an excellent teacher herself, and a good schools minister. She reappointed me as her special adviser on specialist schools. Unfortunately, she felt she had to resign in 2002 when she faced sustained pressure over A-level marking and the vetting of teachers.

Charles Clarke took her place as Secretary of State. Charles had started his political career as head of Neil Kinnock's office and his views on education had reflected his ideas when he was appointed as a junior schools minister to Blunkett's team in 1998. But with responsibility for specialist schools in his brief, his initial scepticism turned to enthusiasm when he returned to the department in the top job. I developed a close relationship with him and was reappointed as his special adviser. Charles lifted the cap in funding of new specialist schools. He wanted all schools to become specialist – and by now they had a dozen specialisms to choose from – so their numbers expanded rapidly from 1,444 in 2003 to over 3,000 in 2009.

Charles Clarke became Home Secretary in December 2004 and Ruth Kelly took his place as Education Secretary and she reappointed me as her special adviser on specialist schools.

Since 1998 I had developed a crucial relationship with Andrew Adonis, who was appointed as Tony Blair's policy adviser on education in 1998 – where he succeeded David Miliband – and subsequently as head of the No. 10 policy unit from 2001 to 2003. This enabled me to develop a good relationship with Tony Blair who came to speak twice at the Annual Conference of the Specialist Schools and Academies Trust as well as visiting specialist schools and CTCs.

I remember taking Andrew to visit the John Kelly Girls' and Boys' Technology Colleges in the London Borough of Brent, which were among the first of the specialist schools established in 1994. Andrew was impressed, and he remained a firm supporter of specialist schools. Andrew, now Lord Adonis, is a highly intellectual and very able person who was a fellow of Nuffield College, Oxford. As a child, he was taken into care, but was fortunate enough to be given a scholarship to attend Kingham Hill boarding school.

Andrew was particularly responsible for the development of the academies programme. Having seen how effective the CTCs were he saw them as a model for reforming urban education, and gained the support of both Blair and Blunkett to develop the idea of the City Academy, later simply shortened to Academy. Academies had similar governance to CTCs, and were funded by Whitehall. They would be non-selective, and initially required £2 million in capital sponsorship, though this requirement was later changed and removed. Andrew worked tirelessly on academies as an adviser and later as schools minister, and felt vindicated when the coalition government expanded the programme after the 2010 election.

In 2004, Tony Blair recommended that I be given the honour of Knight Grand Cross of the Most Excellent Order of the British Empire (GBE) for services to education. Only seven people have been given this honour in the last decade and there are currently only forty members in all. I am one of only a very few people who have two knighthoods.

Following the 2005 election, Andrew was made a peer and appointed schools minister, serving the new Education Secretary Alan Johnson, who reappointed me as special adviser on specialist schools and academies and with whom I developed an excellent relationship. Both specialist schools and academies continued to grow in number with their support.

10

HOW TO RAISE MONEY FOR GOOD CAUSES

When I became chairman of the CTC Trust in 1987, one of my principal duties was to raise £2 million of sponsorship for each of the new City Technology Colleges. I remember vividly my first fund-raising call was to Garry Weston, the chairman of Associated British Foods, one of Britain's largest food companies, and the Garfield Weston Foundation, which is today the second-largest foundation in Britain, awarding £40 million in grants each year. This was an important lesson in fund-raising for me.

An early potential sponsor, Hugh de Capell Brooke, a Northamptonshire landowner, had offered several acres of farmland near Corby on which to build a CTC. However, in order to get approval for the project, we had to raise a further million pounds in cash. After writing hundreds of letters, I received an invitation to meet Garry. His office was in the beautiful Bowater House block of offices in Knightsbridge, which has now been demolished to be replaced by an unattractive block of luxury apartments. I asked how long our meeting would be. He replied, 'As long as necessary.' I explained the need for better technical education in Britain and that Brooke was willing to donate five acres of land for a CTC, as well as how CTCs would work, being independent schools funded by the government. He asked if the CTC Trust was a registered British charity, which it was. After half an hour of discussion, Garry summoned his treasurer to his office and instructed him to give me a cheque for £500,000. I thanked him profusely. I had made a good start as a fund-raiser.

That first successful fund-raising effort taught me three important lessons for the future. The first was that donors will usually only support organisations which are registered charities. The reasons are simple: first they can deduct the donation against their taxes and the charity gets a gift aid supplement from the government. The second is that if you can offer leverage such as government support, it will make your request more attractive. And the third lesson is clearly the most important: the cause must be good. In this case, establishing a great school to teach technical skills in Corby was the deciding factor.

Today the Brooke Weston Academy is one of the finest schools in the country and its federation has sponsored four other academies under the leadership of their outstanding chief executive Sir Peter Simpson. They also supported thirty specialist schools with grants of up to £100,000 each. In total, the Garfield Weston Foundation has contributed £30 million towards the establishment of four CTCs and academies and fifty specialist schools. Quite a result from the first meeting with Garry Weston.

Another great supporter of CTCs, specialist schools and academies has been Lord Harris of Peckham, who was chief executive until 2012 of the Carpetright company that he founded. We first met when we visited incognito, pretending to be quantity surveyors, the failing Sylvan School in Crystal Palace. Phil Harris liked the facilities, so offered to put up the £2 million of sponsorship to convert the school to a CTC. The proposal had to be approved by the parents. Phil and I attended a meeting of 200 parents. Not surprisingly, there was strong support to convert the school to a CTC even though there was a professional political anti-CTC group in the audience. Subsequently, Phil has sponsored eighteen other academies, mainly in South London, which are among the most successful state schools in the country. Led by an outstanding chief executive, Sir Daniel Moynihan, they have developed an approach that brings rapid improvements particularly for disadvantaged pupils. I am privileged to serve as a trustee of the Harris Federation of Schools. The lesson from this sponsor is simple: he liked the idea of funding schools teaching technical skills.

Richard Branson proved an extraordinary sponsor. Today, the Virgin brand is known the world over for everything from airlines and trains to cable TV and megastores. But he started his business empire in the music industry, with the record company that produced many popular 1970s albums and a record store in Oxford Street. Richard told me he wanted to fund a CTC which specialised in teaching the performing arts. But I had to persuade the Prime Minister that this was as valuable as more conventional CTCs which were closer to traditional industries. Today there is widespread recognition of the value of what are now called the creative industries. They employ one in twenty people in the UK and contribute £36 billion a year to the economy, with £4 billion from music, visual and performing arts alone.[10] But in the late eighties, the Prime Minister still took some persuading.

At one meeting in Downing Street, Mrs Thatcher expressed her opposition to the idea by shouting across the cabinet table, 'I don't want to spend taxpayer funds in producing more out-of-work actors.' I had to explain that the purpose of the British Performing Arts School would be to train musicians and singers and teach recording technologies to support the growing recording industry. Mrs Thatcher had initially wanted the record industry to make a greater contribution to what became known as the BRIT School than we expected from sponsors of other CTCs. Fortunately she withdrew her opposition so all we then had to do was find a suitable site. The chief education officer for Croydon suggested we visited the Selhurst School in Croydon, which was failing. When we visited the school, children raced up to Richard asking why he was visiting their school. He said he was going to be their next headmaster.

I became a close friend of Richard and his family, who lived near me in Holland Park. At that time, Richard's only source of income was Virgin Records. But he had great connections and was able to pull together a great line-up for a huge Knebworth outdoor concert on 30 June 1990 which we used to promote the BRIT School. He persuaded famous artists like Paul McCartney, Dire Straits, Eric Clapton, Pink Floyd and Phil Collins to perform, and gained the support of their recording companies including EMI and Chrysalis.

The concert attracted 120,000 people, among them Tony Blair, who was then an opposition spokesman and a keen music fan. Despite the inevitable rain, over £6 million was raised – including through a popular DVD of the event – with some £2.5 million going towards the development of the BRIT School. Over the years, the music industry has donated a total of £7 million to the school.

Today the BRIT School is the most popular performing arts school in the country, with fifteen applications for every place and each applicant has to audition to get in. Among its recent graduates is the very successful singer Adele. In 2011 she earned £13 million from her best-selling recordings and her latest album, 21, has just become the fifth-biggest-selling album of all time. Other successful alumni include Katy B, the late Amy Winehouse, Jessie J, Leona Lewis and The Kooks. The lesson from this is to get on your side a truly outstanding public figure who can bring in other strong support. Raising that money was no mean feat.

Similar examples of extraordinary generosity were shown by Sir Harry Djanogly, who sponsored a CTC in Nottingham, Reg Vardy who created the Emmanuel CTC in Gateshead, Lord Ashworth, who sponsored the ADT College in Wandsworth and Stanley Kalms, the chief executive of Dixons who sponsored the Bradford CTC, and Sir Geoffrey Leigh, who sponsored the Leigh CTC in Dartford. We also had the support of several City Livery Companies, including the Mercers and the Haberdashers, as well as major companies such as Lucas Aerospace, BAT Industries, the Wellcome Trust, Tarmac, the Landau Foundation, Cable & Wireless and the Wolfson Institute. These sponsors together created fifteen CTCs which are now the best state schools in England.

One of the most important reasons for our success in raising funds for the fifteen CTCs was the political support we enjoyed, not least from Baker and Thatcher. The Prime Minister hosted a dinner at No. 10 which proved highly successful in persuading sponsors to support CTCs. Political support was to prove just as important in the academy programme and in raising money for specialist schools. Potential donors want to know they are backing programmes that will stand the test of time.

It is important to give potential donors clear reasons to support your project. I developed a clear brief for sponsors of the new specialist schools. This explained the benefits to the business and to the schools of their sponsorship, and as a result many valuable new links have been developed. Through the Technology Colleges Trust and later the Specialist Schools and Academies Trust we raised £300 million from 600 sponsors for the initiative.

Another important way to raise funds is to understand tax reliefs available for charitable giving through the Gift Aid scheme. In 1992 the Harvard Business School Alumni Club of London, of which I was then the president, became concerned at the decline in the number of British applications for Harvard Business School, which had fallen from twenty-five to just ten, mainly because of the high cost of attending. We decided to set up the British Friends of Harvard Business School as a British registered charity to raise money for tuition scholarships, which we did successfully. We have subsequently raised nearly $3 million in donations. I remember how important it was for me to have a scholarship in the second year of my time at Harvard. So I am delighted that we have been able to join forces with the UK/US Fulbright Commission, with whom we now annually award two or three full tuition scholarships of $50,000 each to financially needy British students.

What has appealed to donors paying UK tax is not only the favourable tax treatment of their donations through the Gift Aid scheme, but also seeing that their donations go directly to funding tuition fees for financially needy students. Donations to the British Friends are deductible under Gift Aid against UK tax, whether or not the donor is a British national, providing that person pays UK taxes. The only requirement is that that donor pays sufficient income or capital gains tax to cover the tax on all his or her donations to UK charities under that scheme and that the donor gives the appropriate certificate if using the Gift Aid scheme. Dual UK/US taxpayers can receive a deduction in both countries if they channel their donation through a body which is recognised in both countries. Charities Aid Foundation American Donor Fund is so structured and the British Friends encourages US donors to donate via that fund. As a British registered charity, the British Friends can also accept donations from other charities.

The chart below illustrates how tax efficient it is for a UK taxpayer to donate to a registered charity:

	Donor gives to charity	Net benefit to charity	Tax gain to charity	Tax benefit to donor	Tax gain	Net cost to donor
Without tax relief	£1,000	£1,000	£NIL	£NIL	£Nil	£1,000
40% tax payer with tax relief	£1,000	£1,250	£250	£250	£500	£750
50% tax payer with tax relief	£1,000	£1,250	£250	£375	£625	£625

Essentially, what happens is this. If someone is a higher-rate taxpayer, paying at the 40 per cent rate, and they donate £1,000, the charity can reclaim an additional £250 from HM Revenue and Customs. At the same time, the donor also receives tax relief that is worth £250, which means that the cost to them of the donation is just £750. There is no additional benefit above the £250 to the charity if the taxpayer pays the rate of 50 per cent (or 45 per cent from 2013) but the donor receives extra tax relief. In the Budget 2012, the Chancellor had initially proposed to cap the level at which higher-rate taxpayers could claim relief, but when George Osborne realised the impact this would have on the charitable sector, he rightly withdrew those proposals.

Fund-raising was a very rewarding task for me. It gave me the chance to meet some great and generous businesspeople, who have become firm friends in the process. But, more importantly, I gained real pleasure visiting the CTCs and schools where sponsors had made such a difference to the lives of children and young people. Through sponsorship, CTCs, specialist schools and academies also gained a fresh perspective and often a new drive that proved important to their improvement. It is important that this energy is maintained as more and more schools become independent of local authority control. Getting that message across was something that I always tried to do as a special adviser to ten secretaries of state.

11

SPECIAL ADVISER

Working for Ten Education Secretaries from 1987 to 2007

Alan Johnson was the tenth successive – and last – Secretary of State for Education to appoint me as their special adviser, a role where I had direct access to them and to key officials to develop the specialist school and academies programme. Kenneth Baker had appointed me initially because he realised that to raise money for CTCs from prospective sponsors and to find sites for their schools would require considerable entrepreneurial skills. He did not believe that many officials would have these skills.

Special advisers have a unique role in British government. Typically, they have considerable influence with the Secretary of State for a particular department as they meet with him or her so frequently – certainly every week. Their role is to warn their Secretary of State about potential political pitfalls and to come up with remedies. Usually a special adviser these days has a private office close to the Secretary of State. But faced with a remote office and no secretarial support, I was pleased with Ken's approval to work out of my own AIFS Queen's Gate office, where I have always had excellent support. I also retained my paid position as chairman of the American Institute for Foreign Study.

I printed new letterheads which showed my office as the office of Kenneth Baker's special adviser on CTCs with the Department of Education logo. This irritated the Permanent Secretary, but there was little he could do while this had the support of the Secretary of State. Uniquely, therefore, although serving in a formal government position, I worked out of my own office. I did not receive a salary although the CTC Trust received a grant to help cover its expenses. I helped Ken to write his speeches and developed a close relationship with him. He allowed me a free hand in finding sponsors and sites for the CTCs. I doubt that, without this freedom to operate, the initiative would have succeeded.

I served ten Secretaries of State over twenty years. A startling fact is that all but three of those Education Secretaries lasted less than two years: Kenneth Baker was in post for three years, as was Gillian Shephard, and David Blunkett was there for four years. More recently, Ed Balls lasted three years but it remains to be seen whether Michael Gove will be in post for the full term. Education is a difficult portfolio, which requires deep knowledge of the subject as well as experience of working with schools. As Education Secretaries appoint their own special advisers, there is also a constant turnover of these people. It is not surprising therefore that, while most Education Secretaries had their good points, the most effective ones, in my view, were Kenneth Baker and David Blunkett.

But it isn't just good ministers who move on too quickly. To get on in the Civil Service, an official is expected to gain experience in as many fields as possible. This means that the best civil servants are moved as soon as they gain expertise in a particular field, though their weaker colleagues often stay where they are. Civil servants are also encouraged to spend time in different departments. We therefore have a worrying lack of continuity at the highest levels of government for both political appointments and civil servants. There are, of course, outstanding exceptions, such as Sir David Bell, whom I found particularly impressive as Permanent Secretary from 2006 to 2011. He brought his experience from teaching, local government and as chief inspector to the role, and has more recently taken up post as the vice-chancellor of Reading University.

The degree of continuity that I enjoyed working with successive education secretaries gave me an enormous advantage in dealing with civil servants, as my files were often better than theirs. More importantly, I knew what had worked and what had not worked in the past. Also, if any Education Secretary wanted to launch a new idea, in many cases I was able to point out that it had been tried and failed before. This long service, experience and knowledge acquired, enabled me to develop close links also with the Prime Minister's policy unit and the No. 10 education advisers.

Under Margaret Thatcher I worked closely with Brian Griffiths, now Lord Griffiths of Fforestfach, who today holds a senior position with Goldman Sachs. He once described me as an 'educational terrorist' because of the way in which CTCs were shaking up the system. I developed similar relationships with Andrew Adonis, Blair's

Above left: 1. My father, Cyril Eustace Taylor, in the Congo in 1927. *Below*: 2. My mother, Marjorie Victoria Hebden, in 1923. *Above right*: 3. Myself at St Marylebone Grammar School in 1947.

Above: 4. Myself as a freshman at Trinity Hall, Cambridge. *Below left*: 5. Myself on our punt, *Ying Tong*, at Cambridge in 1957. *Below right*: 6. Myself at the Taj Mahal.

Right: 7. My wife Judy with our daughter Kirsten. *Below*: 8. My daughter Kirsten, who is a gifted violinist.

Above: 9. My dog Lester. *Right*: 10. My mother, Marjorie Victoria Hebden Taylor, in later life. *Below*: 11. Myself with Prime Minister Ted Heath in the 1974 General Election campaign.

12. Myself after receiving a knighthood from the queen with my wife, Judy, and sister, Sylvia, in 1989.

Above: 13. Myself receiving the award of Knight Grand Cross of the Most Excellent Order of the British Empire from HM the Queen in 2003. *Below*: 14. AIFS's first two offices.

959 Hill Street, Cincinnati, OH　　　　*Temple-Bar Building, Cincinnati, OH*

In 1964 the American Institute For Foreign Study began operating out of an apartment at 959 Hill Street in Cincinnati, Ohio. The company soon moved to the Temple-Bar Building.

American Institute For Foreign Study.
102 GREENWICH AVENUE, GREENWICH, CONNECTICUT 06830
Telephone (203) 869/9090

Above: 15. Senator Robert Kennedy awarding scholarships to AIFS students in 1967.
Below left: 16. The AIFS office at 102 Greenwich Avenue, CT. *Below right*: 17. Myself
with my partner and esteemed friend, Roger Walther.

Above: 18. Richmond, the American International University in London. *Left*: 19. The founders of AIFS: Doug Burck, myself and Roger Walther. *Below left*: 20. The three founders celebrating AIFS's twentieth anniversary with Nell and George Khady.

Above left: 21. The three founders of AIFS meeting at the Vineyard Club, Palm Springs in 2010. *Above right*: 22. Myself welcoming Princess Diana to Richmond, the American International University in London Kensington campus in 1988. *Below*: 23. Senator Jesse Helms congratulating me on the approval of the Au Pair in America programme.

To my distinguished friend, Sir Cyril Taylor, whom I admire greatly!
I hope I will have the good fortune to see you more often.

Jesse Helms, U.S. Senate (N.C.)

24. General Alexander Haig, former Secretary of State and Supreme Allied Commander Europe, whose daughter was at Richmond, greeting myself and Bill Gertz, president of AIFS.

With Best Wishes to Sir Cyril Taylor.
March 3, 2006

Richard G. Lugar
United States Senator

25. Senator Richard Lugar welcoming me to the US Senate in 2006.

26. Michael Portillo receiving an honorary degree from Richmond with Lord Briggs, the chair of governors, and Norman Smith, the president, in 2003.

27. My honorary citizenship conferred by the City of Harrisburg, Pennsylvania in 2009.

28. Myself meeting President Bill Clinton at the Renaissance Conference in 1999.

29. First meeting of the City Technology Colleges Trust in 1988.

Above: 30. Dinner at No. 10 for the CTC sponsors in 1988. *Below, opposite bottom & following four pages*: 32, 33, 34, 35, 36, 37, 38, 39. Cartoons about me and my work published by the TES.

Above: 31. Prime Minister Thatcher welcoming me at No. 10 at CTC Sponsors Dinner in 1988 with Denis Thatcher and Kenneth Baker.

Beg pardon sir, there's a person at the door collecting for a charity called CTC ...

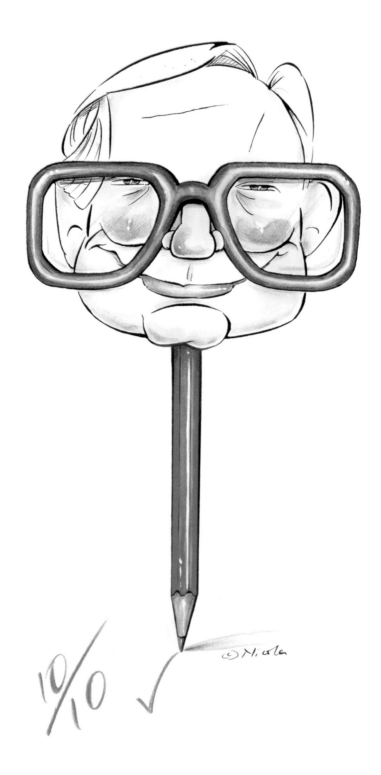

10/10 ✓

SIR . CYRIL TAYLOR   JUNE '00

Super salesman or remote controller?

> PEOPLE BELIEVE IN THEMSELVES BECAUSE WE HAVE THE SPECIALIST MARK... OTHER PEOPLE'S PERCEPTION OF THE SCHOOL HAS CHANGED

40. Prime Minister John Major welcoming me to No. 10.

Left: 41. Myself welcoming Tony Blair, then Leader of the Opposition, to Carmel Technology College in 1996. *Above*: 42. Myself welcoming Prime Minister Blair to the Specialist Schools and Academies Trust National Conference. *Below*: 43. Prime Minister Blair together with Charles Clarke, Secretary of State for Education, and myself welcoming Larry Ellison, chairman of Oracle, to No. 10.

Left: 44. Note of thanks from Prime Minister Blair to me on the publication of our joint paper. *Above*: 45. Lord Adonis and Lord Baker with Baroness Thatcher celebrating the publication of a study of specialist schools. *Below*: 46. Myself thanking Baroness Thatcher for her support.

Above: 47. Lord Baker, David Blunkett MP, Lord Adonis and George Weston at the launch of my book, *A Good School for Every Child*, in 2009. *Left*: 48. Myself with Prime Minister Gordon Brown. *Below*: 49. Myself as High Sheriff of Greater London in 1996 making an award. *Opposite*: 50. The Queen Mother visiting Lexham Gardens in 1996.

Above, below right & opposite: 52–4. Lexham Gardens as it is today.

Lot 18

Lexham Gardens, Kensington, London W8

Freehold ½ acre Garden Square in Central London – Underground Development Potential Subject to Necessary Consents

Tenure
Freehold.

Location
Lexham Gardens is located just to the north of Cromwell Road in a highly sought after residential area between Harlees Road and "Point West" (formerly the West London Air Terminal) currently being redeveloped for residential purposes.

Description
The property comprises the Garden Square overlooked by the impressive residential properties of Lexham Gardens, and extends in all to approximately ½ acre.

Relevant Statutes
The use of the gardens is subject to two Acts of Parliament, namely the Kensington Improvement

Act 1851 and the London Square Preservation Act 1931, which inter alia limit access to the property to those occupiers who overlook the gardens and all persons to whom such owner shall have granted or may hereafter grant a Right of Access. There is provision for maintenance and management by a Gardens Committee (made up of qualifying occupiers) recovering the outgoings by way of a rates supplement levied on those qualifying occupiers. The freeholder thereby incurs no outgoings and accrues no income and thus no management. No restriction is placed on the owner or lessee of such a Square from carrying out underground works.

Tenancy
The entire property is offered with FULL VACANT POSSESSION upon completion, subject to statutes detailed above.

Vendor's Solicitor
R. Caplan, Esq.
Robert Gore & Co.
17 Grosvenor Street
London W1X 9FD
Tel: 01-491 2020
Fax: 01-499 6123

Vacant Possession on Completion

(subject to statute)

PAGE THIRTY-THREE

Left: 51. Lexham Gardens as it looked in 1990.

Above: 55. Lunch at St James's Palace hosted by HRH The Duke of Edinburgh for the GBE knights. *Left*: 56. Myself in GBE regalia in March 2012.

brilliant adviser, and with Conor Ryan, who succeeded Andrew as Blair's education adviser in 2005. These relationships were crucial, especially with the turnover of Education Secretaries being so great. I could not have converted the vast majority of English secondary schools into specialist schools or kick-started the academies movement without their support.

My close relationship with No. 10 also greatly helped my work on the CTCs and specialist schools and academies. It was an important way of engaging and thanking sponsors, and of ensuring that the programmes had the drive they often needed from the centre of government. This special relationship enabled me to persuade Margaret Thatcher to hold a Downing Street dinner for the fifteen CTC sponsors in 1988. I have described how the decision to expand the specialist programme was taken with John Major in 1996. After the change to a Labour government, Andrew Adonis arranged for John Chambers, the president of Cisco Systems Inc., the multinational information technology firm, and me to meet with Tony Blair to discuss setting up Cisco academies in English schools, where students could learn vital IT skills. Similarly, he arranged for Charles Clarke, then the Education Secretary, and me to meet with the Prime Minister Tony Blair and Larry Ellison, chairman of Oracle, to set up Oracle academies. On this occasion, we were ushered into Tony Blair's small private office. When the Prime Minister asked me to start the discussion, I explained that Oracle had agreed in principle to establish 200 Oracle academies in English schools and we were meeting to discuss the proposal. Larry Ellison interrupted me to say that 200 was too small a number and suggested 1,000. Such is the heady effect of visiting Downing Street.

However, my status as a special adviser was not always an asset. In 2006, the *Sunday Times* had extended its investigations into 'cash for honours' – at a time when the police were looking into claims that party donors could 'buy' peerages – into suggestions that there was a direct relationship between the sponsorship of academies and the receipt of an honour such as a knighthood or a peerage. Of course, many of those who were sponsors were philanthropists and honours were often given for supporting charitable causes. Despite months of police investigations, they never found any evidence to show that honours were being 'sold' in the way that the newspaper alleged. Unfortunately, one of the trustees of the Specialist Schools and Academies Trust, Desmond Smith, who was a very able headteacher of a Catholic school in East London, was trapped by one of the newspaper's reporters into saying that sponsors of academies would be likely to be rewarded with an honour. Those words were to cost a good man dear, and he found himself arrested by the police, and forced to resign his job. Of course, he was cleared of any wrongdoing, yet a good man and a brilliant headteacher had his life and career ruined in the process. It was terribly tragic.

Two reporters from the *Sunday Times* tried the same trick with me by posing as prospective sponsors. Although I was suspicious of them, after many phone calls, I finally agreed to have lunch with them at L'Orange Restaurant in St James's Street. I was immediately suspicious when the female reporter placed her handbag on the table, assuming that it must contain a microphone. I explained how the academy sponsorship worked and was asked if they agreed to sponsor an academy, whether the sponsor would receive a knighthood? I replied that to make such a promise would be corrupt and terminated the lunch.

Of course, it is right for newspapers to be on their guard against genuinely corrupt practice. But the problem with the constant attacks on those who choose to give generously of their time and money to charitable causes like education is that it makes them reluctant to contribute. Sponsorship was a vital element of CTCs and academies particularly, as the drive that the philanthropic sponsors bring to the project is essential in galvanising early and sustained improvements. Fortunately, the constant questioning of their motivation has not deterred determined sponsors such as Lord Harris, whose academies now educate 11,600 children mainly in South London and whose federation aims to include twenty-five primary and secondary academies. Thanks to his leadership and the great team he has around him, Harris Academies continue to improve at a remarkable rate.

What, then, are the key attributes of a successful special adviser? They should have specialist knowledge of the area or responsibility for the department in which they are working. Advisers must be able to give ministers informed advice on the proposals of officials. They must have good inter-personal skills in dealing with a wide range of people, including politicians, officials, the press and Members of Parliament. They must be able to write draft speeches as well as giving written advice to their minister. They should have experience in dealing with the media. And, perhaps most crucial of all, special advisers must be very discreet and be careful to keep their inside knowledge confidential.

In the Spotlight
Sometimes, it was not so good being in the spotlight. Combining a role of special adviser and chairman of the trust meant that I had come to attention of the influential chairman of the Education Select

Committee in the House of Commons. Barry Sheerman, Labour MP for Huddersfield, whom I got to know well, had first been elected as MP for the old Huddersfield East constituency in 1979, five years after I had unsuccessfully contested the seat. As chair of the select committee, he ensured that it became an increasingly powerful check on government and I was invited to give evidence on several occasions. But he was always quick to pick up on my occasional media appearances, where I sometimes courted controversy. In late 2005, I gave evidence on trust schools along with Elizabeth Reid, who was chief executive of the SSAT and Liz Sidwell, then head of Haberdashers' Aske's (and now Schools Commissioner). But I had recently been talking up my ideas for identifying the top 5 per cent of pupils to ensure their abilities were recognised in comprehensive schools, and this seemed to fit with the concerns of some Labour MPs that trust schools were something to do with selection.

Barry Sheerman was in full flight as he challenged me. 'Here are you coming and saying that what you want is great collaboration, groups of schools and confederations of schools, and we have heard that before, but round about the same time you were appearing in the national press calling for the 5 per cent of brightest children to be identified at ten or eleven and fast-tracked through the education system. That is even more radical than bringing grammar schools back, is it not?' Of course it was not, and I assured him and the committee that the opposite was the case: academies like CTCs were comprehensive schools that were required to be non-selective; the same would be the case with trust schools.

Perhaps it was unwise to talk so freely to the press, particularly as my role was seen as so close to ministers, yet I felt it important to air issues on radio and television, including the *Today* programme. My increasing knowledge of the continuing weaknesses in the English education system meant that I felt there were times that I had to speak out, even where it might provoke a backlash. For example, in 2007, I drew attention to the extreme difficulty in getting rid of ineffective teachers, of whom I estimated, using Ofsted data, there were at least 17,000, out of a total of 425,000 teachers, of which only ten had been let go in the previous three years. The National Union of Teachers, who were often in denial about the scale of the problem, said they couldn't understand where I had got my figures from. Behind the scenes, there were some concerns from ministers too, as they felt the publicity distracted from their efforts to work more closely with the unions. But I still feel it is better to air these issues than simply to talk about them behind closed doors.

This prominence also led to some interviews, including that by Peter Wilby, which he has adapted at the start of this book. But I fear this particular article, which perhaps exaggerated my influence and importance, created difficulties with the Civil Service and Elizabeth Reid, the dynamic SSAT chief executive, who would have preferred me to have a lower profile.

New Governments, Changing Role

I had been a special adviser for twenty years to ten education secretaries when Tony Blair resigned as Prime Minister in 2007. He sent me a very kind letter thanking me for my contribution. The Chancellor of the Exchequer Gordon Brown was his successor in No. 10, and he moved Alan Johnson from Education to Health. Brown's close associate, Ed Balls, was appointed to the education job, though the department was split, with universities and colleges hived off to the business department, and what had been the Department for Education and Skills renamed the Department for Children, Schools and Families.

With a change in name there was a big change in attitude. Brown and Balls had been sceptical initially about academies, but they kept Andrew Adonis as schools minister which ensured that the academies expansion continued apace. Naturally, I indicated I would be honoured to continue to serve as the special adviser for specialist schools and academies. But I received a friendly, but disappointing letter from David Bell saying that Ed Balls would be unable to reappoint me as his special adviser because No. 10 had decided that each Secretary of State should have no more than two special advisers and Ed Balls preferred to have two full-time special advisers. Since I was not paid for my services, and therefore did not count as a government employee, this hardly seemed a reasonable explanation. Probably the real reason was that both No. 10 and Ed Balls felt I was too closely associated with Tony Blair. Gordon Brown did, however, write me a very kind letter expressing appreciation for my public service since 1987.

I continued to serve as chair of the SSAT overseeing a major review of its governance. The CTC Trust that had started to serve a relatively small number of schools had grown to embrace some 3,000 specialist schools, a growing number of primary and special schools, and an increasing membership outside England. It was also receiving a growing number of government contracts to deliver key school improvement programmes, and had revenues approaching £100 million. The Charity Commission, not unreasonably, felt that this required more robust internal governance, and that a board of trustees with twenty-four members was too large.

A meeting of existing trustees was held in October 2007 and the reformed governance structure was approved, which reduced the number of trustees to twelve, while retaining a larger advisory council. I also believed that I was formally reappointed chair of trustees at this meeting on a motion moved by David Samworth. I was therefore surprised when at a special meeting of the new board of trustees in December 2007 to elect the officers for the coming year it was decided to invite applications to become the new chair.

The deputy chairman, Sir James Hill, had decided – or been persuaded – to stand against me. Both of us were asked to leave the room while the remaining trustees decided how to vote. The discussion lasted for two hours. I had accepted that a change in the chair of the SSAT might be desirable, but had hoped and asked to remain for one final year, after which time I would retire. Sir James was elected chairman in my place.

I had to make a choice. Should I express my disappointment at my treatment and resign from the trust, or say nothing and remain as a trustee to help in any way that I could under the new chairman? This was the trust that I had started twenty years before, and I still felt it was an important part of me. I decided that personal feelings should be set aside. I refused numerous requests for press interviews and declined to criticise what had happened.

When Andrew Adonis called me over the Christmas holiday to express his regret at my departure, I told him that I had decided to put the interests of the children in the 3,000 specialist schools first, and not cause any trouble. This was appreciated by the trust, who held a dinner in my honour following the annual sponsors' reception in January 2008 at the Guildhall, at which I was invited to make a farewell speech. Ed Balls attended and thanked me for my service. Sir James resigned the chairmanship a year later and was succeeded by Nick Stuart, a distinguished former civil servant.

I was very proud of having helped to make the SSAT one of the leading education charities in the world. I decided to write a book on my twenty years' service as chair of the trust, which I did with able help and research by Christine Walter (Prentice), formerly my policy advisor, and Jane Ware. Hannelore Fuller, my personal assistant, had the unenviable task of typing the handwritten 300-page document, as she has done for this book. The book, *A Good School for Every Child*, was published by Routledge in February 2009. The

Weston Foundation, with whom I have a close relationship, paid a substantial grant so that a copy could be sent to the headteachers of every secondary school. I was particularly pleased that the two Education Secretaries for whom I had the most admiration, Lord Baker of Dorking and David Blunkett, kindly agreed to provide a rare bipartisan joint introduction. Lord Rees, the President of the Royal Society and Astronomer Royal, described the book as 'so much important good sense expressed so cogently and with such authority'. The book was launched at the Institute of Economic Affairs in 2009 with Lord Baker, David Blunkett, George Weston and Lord Adonis as the guests of honour.

By the autumn of 2009, David Cameron was riding high as leader of the Conservative Party. The economic crisis of 2008 had left Gordon Brown politically damaged, and it seemed likely that Labour would lose the next General Election. I therefore had a number of meetings with the new Shadow Education Secretary, Michael Gove. Gove was a former *Times* journalist who had a keen interest in education reform. He decided early on, for example, to embrace the idea of academies rather than increasing selective education and regarded the changes he planned as a radical form of Blairism. At a Carlton Club lunch, held in June 2009, with Gove and some fifteen specialist school and academy principals and sponsors, a valuable discussion took place. I prepared four papers with a number of recommendations for an incoming Conservative government on how they might advance the specialist schools and academies programmes. Gove said he strongly supported most of the recommendations.

As expected, Labour was defeated in the May 2010 General Election. Gove was appointed Education Secretary in the coalition government formed by David Cameron and Nick Clegg in May 2010. He quickly restored the title of Department of Education and started a rapid expansion of academies, introducing legislation to make it easier for any primary, secondary or special school to convert to academy status with DfE approval. They would not need sponsorship to do so, though they would be expected to work in partnership with other schools and would receive a proportion of local authority funds as they would now be directly funded by Whitehall. Automatic approval was given to schools rated outstanding or good with outstanding features by Ofsted. After the first year, with Liz Sidwell as his Schools Commissioner, he gave new life to the sponsored academy programme – nearly 280 had been planned by the 2010 election, and he now focused on failing primaries as well as secondaries. By August 2012, nearly 2,000 primary and secondary schools had become academies.

The original fifteen City Technology Colleges, on which academies are based, have thus proved their worth.

But Gove was less keen on specialist schools. With over 90 per cent of schools having specialist status and strong budgetary pressures, he decided to stop providing separate funding to specialist schools. Any funding they had received would go through a single school budget in future. Schools would be free to maintain their specialism – and most have chosen to do so. I could not understand why the coalition had made this change. Specialist schools had transformed the system in a number of ways, notably in their improvement of school leadership, hailed recently by the OECD as the best in the developed world. They had been a force for good in promoting their specialist subjects, including computers in schools, modern languages and sports. And their focus on accountability had undoubtedly helped to raise standards, with the proportion of pupils gaining five good GCSE grades including English and Maths rising from a third to over half.

System leadership was at the heart of what the SSAT gave to English education. Now, more than ever, it is in demand as the government rightly sets increasingly challenging floor targets. But it has limited the number of agencies to help provide that system leadership. And the SSAT was a victim of this decision. The premature withdrawal of an annual £20 million government grant to the trust led to what was by that stage known as the Schools Network having to sell its overseas contracts – it had developed programmes in the Middle East and China – and to appoint administrators. The SSAT was able to survive thanks to a management buyout, led by Sue Williamson. It still has 5,000 member schools worldwide and has an important role to play in spreading best practice. I hope that it continues to be a strong force for school improvement in its latest incarnation.

12

HIGH SHERIFF

High Sheriff of Greater London, Working with Young Offenders, Improving Literacy & Cutting Unemployment

After the abolition of the GLC in 1996, I was greatly privileged to be appointed by Her Majesty the Queen as the High Sheriff of Greater London for a year. In theory, the High Sheriff is responsible for the administration of justice in the capital including the police, the prisons and the courts. In practice, the position, which dates back to Saxon times, is mainly honorary. The Greater London office had been created in 1965. During my period of office, I visited all the city's prisons, sat beside judges when offenders were tried and accompanied the police on their night patrols. In the process, I learned a great deal about the administration of law and order in the capital.

Because of my interest in the welfare and education of young people, I decided to focus on learning how to improve our treatment of young offenders as well as on how we can reduce crime committed by young people. I made several visits to the young offenders' prison in Feltham, in West London. I insisted on meeting prisoners with just an attendant present to open and shut cell doors, but without the head warden. As the High Sheriff, I had the right to do this, even though some assumed the position was purely ceremonial. I believed that visiting the cells in this way would give me a fuller picture of what conditions were like.

I was right and I had some amazing discussions. In one of the first cells I went into, a really hardened young criminal was sharing with another young man who was simply on probation awaiting trial, and who had not yet been found guilty. Effectively these probationers were in a school of crime, often having to wait up to a year to go to trial. At least this has since been improved, with offenders having to be brought to court within ninety days. But at that time as many as a third of the prisoners at Feltham were awaiting trial, which was completely wrong. On a more positive note, one of the wardens told me how one young offender, on leaving prison and who was trying to turn his life around, would regularly telephone him to update him on progress and this warden effectively acted as a surrogate parent giving advice and encouragement.

A disproportionate share of crime is committed by young men. Those under eighteen commit nearly a quarter of all crimes even though they make up just one tenth of the population, according to Home Office estimates. The vast majority of these crimes – 860,000 out of 1,020,000 – were committed by males.[11] Half of all robberies are committed by young people in this age group. In 2010/11, a total of 176,511 proven offences were committed by young people, and 2,040 are held in custody at any one time. The Commission on Youth Crime and Anti-Social Behaviour, funded by the Nuffield Foundation, has estimated the cost of police and justice for young offenders to be around £4 billion a year.[12] These young offenders often enter a pipeline to a life of crime, with 75 per cent re-offending within two years.

This is why we end up spending so much on our prisons. The prison budget used to be equal to one fifth of the total education budget. Even today, the Ministry of Justice, which administers the criminal justice system by funding courts, prisons and legal aid, costs £8.9 billion each year, nearly a quarter of the total schools budget. Crime is therefore a very expensive business for the taxpayer. Re-offending rates are also high. Too many prisoners, released prematurely from prison because of the muddle over remand times, re-offend within a few days of their release.

As High Sheriff, the only bright spot was that the rate of re-offending dropped sharply when offenders reached their mid-thirties. But a figure I found most startling was that the National Crime Survey estimated that less than half of all crimes were reported to the police, only one third were recorded, and only 3 in 100 crimes resulted in a caution or conviction. This data led criminologists to the conclusion that many of the 60,000 people in prison at that time were likely to form a permanent criminal class, to whom prison served neither as a deterrent nor as a source of rehabilitation. Increasingly its principal purpose became the protection of society by removing criminals from circulation.

When I spoke to prisoners, many of them told me that sentences did not deter them from re-offending, and that only increasing the chances of detection would do so. I concluded we needed to do much more to prevent crime from happening in the first place. Every crime prevented means one less victim. This also saves the huge cost of catching and dealing with the offender. If we had not then done more to prevent crime in the first place, we faced the real prospect of an explosive increase in the size of the prison population and a commensurate increase in the cost of the prison service.

For example, in the United States, a country of some 300 million people, there are 2,267,000 people in prison.[13] This is a proportion nearly five times the level in the United Kingdom. I calculated that if we had had a similar proportion of people in prison in the UK, the numbers in prison would increase to 438,000 people at a cost of £17 billion.

An increase in the numbers of people in prison of this proportion is clearly unacceptable; few would want Britain to become a gulag society. This is why I became attracted to different ways of preventing crime, particularly the reduction of young offending. I believed that this would be more effective, more socially beneficial and less expensive than alternatives like better policing or stricter sentencing policies. I had been appointed High Sheriff the year after the headteacher Philip Lawrence was murdered by young members of a local gang as he tried to stop trouble at the gates of his Maida Vale school. His widow Frances Lawrence, a woman of great dignity, pleaded for more to be done to stop the rise in the number of young offenders. While some progress may have been made in the intervening years, I believe we still need to do much more to prevent crime by young people.

We need to learn more about the causes of the rise in the number of young offenders. Research indicates that many young offenders share common origins and traits. The majority are boys who have suffered from inadequate parenting and attend poor schools or were excluded from school at an early age. They have poor reading and numeracy skills (and thus find it difficult to find jobs), come from single parent families living in inner-city stress areas, and 70 per cent of those under supervision by the Probation Service are out of work. Many have become involved in drugs or alcohol abuse. Nearly all have very low self-esteem and many mix with other offenders. There is a clear link between poverty, unemployment and a general disenchantment with society, which leads to drug abuse and so criminalises many who would not otherwise become offenders.

After her husband's murder, Frances Lawrence published a manifesto, where she stressed the importance teaching children at school the difference between right and wrong, placing more emphasis on the crucial role played by parents and the importance of family life, giving a higher status to teachers and requiring primary school lessons in good citizenship to be taught. The Philip Lawrence Awards remain a fitting tribute to that brave headmaster in promoting good citizenship to young people.

Back in 1996, I was particularly struck by an Audit Commission report, *Misspent Youth*, which said that any strategy for tackling youth crime must address the behaviour of four different groups of young people: persistent offenders; young offenders who had yet to develop an entrenched pattern of offending; first-time offenders and, finally, and probably most important, young people at risk such as those who are excluded from schools and need to be discouraged from offending in the first place. The report argued that measures such as mandatory counselling on good parenting, improved remedial education and counselling for those excluded from schools including improving the special referral units for those persistently excluded from school and greater involvement was needed by the voluntary sector, including the churches, in providing support and mentoring centres such as the Foundation Centre in Wandsworth.

Since then, there has been a welcome move towards establishing better units for excluded pupils, including studio schools, with more receiving a full-time education, and parenting orders have been introduced too. The Youth Justice Board has taken very effective action in helping young offenders. As a result, fewer young offenders are in custody and the rate of re-offending by young people is lower than when I was High Sheriff. But I believe we need to treat this as a much greater issue than it has been by successive governments. Not to do so would be to fail future generations.

The ever-present danger was highlighted in the summer of 2011, when we had the devastating outbreak of riots in our major cities. Shops were destroyed. People's livelihoods were wrecked, and there was mayhem on the streets for several days. That may have been a rare incident, but it highlighted the need to redouble our efforts to tackle youth crime. Two crucial ways to do this are by reducing illiteracy and unemployment.

We Need a Reading Revolution

When I enrolled at Harvard Business School in September 1959 I was given a reading test. The school said the test showed I was a slow reader and that slow readers do not understand what they are reading as well as fast readers. As a result, I was required to take the Evelyn Wood Rapid Reading Course. This teaches you to scan paragraphs to get the meaning of the text rather than spelling out each word. Consequently you understand the context much better. Fast reading with good comprehension has proved a most valuable skill and helped me in my career. For example, I was, to the surprise of civil servants, able to read long policy papers very quickly and advise the Secretary of State on their contents.

However, it is much more serious if you cannot read at all. On my visits to young offenders' institutions as High Sheriff, I quickly discovered that a key reason why so many young people ended up there was their inability to read and write adequately, or at all. And the truth is that even though there has been a great improvement in literacy levels in recent years, too many of our children still do not know how to read sufficiently well. In 2007, I gave a lecture to the Royal Society of Arts on this theme, and many of the issues I identified today remain relevant, although the greater use of synthetic phonics to help children decode words is beginning to have an impact in primary schools, and the current schools minister David Laws is right to encourage its use through the new National Curriculum.

Eighteen per cent of English eleven-year-olds did not gain a level four – the expected level for their age – in the national tests in 2011. These 100,000 children will find it very difficult to access the secondary curriculum, and though they should receive remedial teaching at secondary school, they will start with a significant disadvantage. But those figures don't even tell the whole story. The figures are worse for boys: 23 per cent fall below level four and 31 per cent don't make the grade for writing. One figure I discovered when preparing my RSA speech was that the 2005 National Reading Campaign survey had found that 20 per cent of the children taking part reported their parents did not help them to read. Poor literacy may be being transferred across generations.

These worrying statistics are of even greater concern because literacy is so important to general learning. An estimated 75 per cent of academic success is predicted by reading ability. As David Blunkett said when he launched his successful literacy strategy in 1997, 'If you can't read, you can't learn.' Or learn much history. Even science and maths ability depend on one's ability to read. If you can't read the maths problem you can't solve it. Children must know how to read in order to be able to read to learn.

Not being able to read leads to boredom at school, truancy, and sometimes worse things, especially for boys. On a visit to St Paul's Elementary School in a very poor area of Harlem in New York, a school which has exceptional reading test scores, I found primary school children reading two grade levels higher than similar children in other schools in Harlem. I found it an inspirational school. All the children read books. The school set aside an hour a day for supervised silent reading in school. The students were reading lots of books, and the reason they were doing so was due both to the teachers and to a program called the Accelerated Reader designed by Renaissance Learning. Students would read a book and as soon as they finished they would run to the computer to take the Accelerated Reader comprehension quiz. Quiz scores were posted on the walls of the classroom. Inevitably, all the children insisted I take a quiz, too. So I skimmed a short children's book, called *Three Crocodiles and an Island*, took the AR test, and got only three out of five questions right. The children danced around shouting with great glee, 'He got two wrong!'

But these children showed what can be done and they are not isolated examples. Primary schools in the London borough of Tower Hamlets, one of the poorest areas in the country, reach the national average in English, thanks to a strong emphasis on phonics, and across Inner London, a similarly strong focus means that children now do better than the rest of the country. Once they have decoded words through phonics, it is essential for children to read a lot of books to become good at reading. The research confirms what common sense suggests. Students who score in the top 5 per cent on standardised reading tests read 144 times more than students who score in the bottom 5 per cent. A 2002 study by the OECD (Organisation for Economic Co-operation and Development) of 174,000 students in thirty-two countries showed time spent reading books is the single best predictor of academic achievement, more highly correlated to success than even socio-economic status or ethnicity.

The Rose Review recommendations adopted by the Department for Education and Skills in 2005 – and the subsequent promotion of phonics by the coalition government – were a major step forward because it is essential that we teach children how to read phonetically, how to decode letters and sound words out. But as Jim Rose, the report's author and a former Director of Inspection at Ofsted, said, teaching students to read words is just the first step in encouraging students to read a lot and to understand what they are reading. Acquiring word recognition skills through a good phonics programme should be a time limited accomplishment with hopefully all seven-year-olds having achieved this. Failure to learn to decode and encode print leaves children demotivated, floundering and in need of expensive catch-up programmes.

In addition to encouraging children to read books, it is essential for them to have time at school to read books. I was lucky to have plenty of books at home. Indeed, I used to read avidly under the bedclothes with a torch when my mother turned off the light. Those Harlem students at St Paul's may not have books at home, but they have school that provides them instead.

I may be sounding my age a little, but I do feel lucky not to have had all the distractions that kids have today. I was astonished to hear that in the typical home in England the TV and the computer are on over seven hours per day!

Many students who are behind in their reading are not going to read at home because there are often no books at home and the TV is on or they are using their laptops to send messages via social media such as Facebook. To develop good readers, there must be time set aside during the school day for students to read books. And time at school for reading books is just as important in secondary schools as in primary schools.

The visit to the Harlem primary school was a revelation but I've learned over the years to maintain a sceptical attitude, and as chairman of the Specialist Schools and Academies Trust my main interest at that time was in secondary schools.

In that capacity, in early 2005, I visited the Ammons Middle School, in a socially disadvantaged area of Miami, Florida. Ammons has around 1,100 students aged between eleven and thirteen, with 52 per cent of its pupils Hispanic and 26 per cent African American. Yet, under the leadership of principal Irwin Adler, the Ammons Middle School won numerous awards for test score improvement and parental involvement. Of Ammons' eighth-grade students, 86 per cent score at or above grade level because of the Accelerated Reader programme compared to around half of other Florida eighth graders. They set aside a forty-five-minute teaching period every day when all students do nothing but read in their classroom. It was so amazing during reading time at 8.30 in the morning to see every single child reading a book. And it was so quiet that you could have heard a pin drop.

A little later I realised this approach had started to catch on in the UK as well. Kathy Heaps, at the time head at John Kelly Girls' Technology College in Brent – where I took Andrew Adonis for our first meeting – who was using the Accelerated Reader, told me that children in her inner-city school were hooked on books. Library circulation had rocketed and, much to the librarian's glee, so did the book budget. The library was busy, and to this day it still is. In fact, they have moved computers out of the library to fit more books in. As was true at Ammons, Kathy had invested in the books needed and had a full-time librarian. They started with only 3,000 books and they now have over 16,000 books in the John Kelly Girls' school library. How many secondary schools in England have 16,000 books in their libraries? Only one third has a qualified librarian and a further third have a teacher with library skills, but one third have neither. A report by the charity Bookstart found that primary schools spend only £8 per pupil per year on books, and secondary schools only spend £3. Many school libraries don't allow children to take books out on loan.

These examples reinforced my belief in the importance of individual personalised reading and learning. Students should be able to choose their own books with the help of the teacher and the librarian. They should be encouraged to read whole texts. The teacher made sure the books were within the students' respective reading level as determined by the Star test, so every student was assured of success at their individual level.

But I was still unsure whether or not the Accelerated Reader and Star products would work in other secondary schools in England. The only way SSAT or I could support the use of Renaissance products would be to see them proven in England's secondary schools. That's why we piloted them in 2005. At the same time, Renaissance Learning made the commitment to fully Anglicise their online comprehension tests. So far, 10,000 have been anglicised, but there are a further 100,000 books where this needs to happen. The Star products have even been adapted to provide equivalent key stage test scores aligned to the English National Curriculum. This was an another excellent example of transatlantic education working well.

The National Foundation for Educational Research reported that the pilots went very well. Over six months, the average reading age increased by 40 per cent above the expected growth, though children were only spending around fifteen minutes a day on supervised silent reading, which was not enough. Nevertheless, children loved the 'book in the bag' idea at the heart of the programme, and all the pilot schools renewed their contract with Renaissance Learning and extended it to include even more of their students. Over 1,000 English schools are now using Accelerated Reader, including many academies.

Of course, tackling illiteracy is not easy, but I think we now know what works. First, we need to teach students how to read, using phonics, how to decode and sound out words, but that is just the beginning. Then we need to motivate students to read a lot of books. The amount of book reading students do directly translates into improved academic performance in all subjects. thirty minutes of independent, supervised silent book reading practice per day at school should be the minimum for secondary schools, perhaps as much as sixty minutes for primary school, and the pupils need to take short quizzes on their comprehension. Many of the students we most want to help do not read at home. Many homes in socially disadvantaged areas have no books at home and the TV is on over seven hours a day.

But this won't work unless we have sufficient books in school libraries to support half an hour of reading each day. A good library would have at least ten books for every student, on average 10,000 books in a secondary school with a suitable range of books appropriate for the age range in the school. For this to work well, all secondary schools need a full-time qualified librarian, or at least a teacher with librarian skills, and the library needs to be at the heart of the learning experience. A 2005 Loughborough University study found a 23 per cent drop in professional library staff in the schools' library service with seven in ten fourteen-year-olds not actively using, or being a member of, any public library service. Ofsted has shown the strong correlation between well-funded libraries with full-time librarians and exceptional results.

For students to be motivated and book reading to be effective, literacy improvement must be personalised, individualised and accountable, with children being encouraged to read, to understand and to later take comprehension quizzes. But all this requires skilled enthusiastic headteachers and teachers having the ability to make data driven decisions. It is the teacher who uses the data to interact with students who make the difference. And it takes an enthusiastic headteacher who insists on fully funding the library, gets the teachers the training they need, and assures there is a sufficient in-school reading time every day to create the culture of reading which will solve the literacy problem.

Everyone can benefit. This approach works well, not only with poor readers, but good readers too. But for poor readers to benefit, it is important that their reading needs are identified with a reading test when they start secondary school. The national tests taken in primary school often fail to provide a full picture. Children who are diagnosed as having a reading problem will need special coaching and good schools will teach them how to read in the first year at secondary school with a test to verify this has been accomplished. If necessary, the normal timetable for these children should be suspended until they have learned to read. What is not acceptable is for the children to pass through secondary school and to leave school unable to read properly. That is a stepping stone for too many to a life of crime and unemployment.

Reducing Youth Unemployment

Twenty-one per cent of young people in Britain aged sixteen to twenty-four are not in employment, education or training – that's 1,134,000 young people. A significant proportion of them have not had any work at all since leaving school, and lack the skills needed to gain regular employment. I found as High Sheriff how close the links between unemployment and crime could be.

With a higher participation age by 2015, all seventeen- and eighteen-year-olds should at least be receiving some training, even if they are not still at school or college. But too often it is excessive regulation that makes it too difficult for employers to give young people a chance. I was impressed by a superb 2011 paper by Dominic Raab MP for the Centre of Policy Studies on the subject. I think that the coalition should embrace his recommendations and conclusions.

Raab demonstrated that the burden of employment regulation in the UK has swollen six times over the last thirty years. In 2011, UK business spent £112 billion on compliance costs – the equivalent of 7.9 per cent of GDP. He suggested that another £23 billion in costs on business will be imposed by 2015. For small businesses, the costs of compliance are disproportionately high, often crushing the spirit of enterprise out of small business. Higher levels of employment regulation put the entitlements and rights of the employed above the plight of the unemployed. He argued – rightly, in my experience – that reducing the burden of employment regulation will help businesses to regain the confidence essential for economic growth and job creation.

Raab made a series of proposals that he argues would go a long way to reducing regulatory burdens. He would exclude start-ups, micro- and small businesses from key regulations. The minimum wage of those under twenty-one is £4.98 an hour since October 2012, whereas those employing apprentices aged nineteen or under only have to pay £2.65 an hour. Exempting these small firms from the under-twenty-one wage would allow them to give more young people a chance. He would also exempt these firms from the extension of flexible working regulations, requests for time off for training and from pension auto-enrolment (which will affect them from 2015).

A major deterrent to employers giving young people a chance is that it will prove difficult to dismiss them if they are not up to the job. Tribunals can be particularly expensive for small firms. Raab suggests several measures here, including no-fault dismissal for under-performing employees, stronger powers for employment tribunals to strike out and deter spurious claims, a qualified registrar to pre-vet tribunal claims and the promotion of arbitration and other alternative dispute resolutions. Raab's other proposals are to promote flexible working for senior employees and manage the Default Retirement Age; to require a majority of support from balloted members for any strike in the emergency and transport sectors; to reform TUPE – the Transfer of Undertakings (Protection of Employment) – regulations where employees keep their existing rights if their business is taken over to encourage business rescues and to promote successful business models; and to abolish the Agency Workers Regulations 2010 and the Working Time Regulations 1998, both of which impact on small firms.

These measures would help the Coalition government meet the Chancellor's aspiration of clearing every obstacle to growth. But the reasons for youth unemployment have several other explanations. The first is historical. The Butler 1944 Education Act[14] was never properly implemented. While a third of the population were well-educated in the selective grammar schools, many of the rest did not receive a good education in the secondary modern schools, and no more than 200 technical schools were established. By contrast, the English education experts who advised Germany on how to establish a similar system in 1945 did a much better job – and the Germans have a highly rated vocational and apprenticeship system.

A second crucial cause is the fact that over half of English-maintained secondary schools do not have a sixth form.[15] Every year, over 300,000 sixteen-year-olds have to transfer to another school, sixth-form college or further education college. While sixth-form colleges offer good specialist teaching for A-levels, many go to very large further education colleges which are often unable to provide the pastoral support which students of this age group require. These are often the students who need most support, often to retake GCSEs. As a result, the drop-out rate of FE students is very high – over a fifth do not complete their courses successfully. Overall in 2007, only 317,000 students took either A-levels or other Level 3 examinations out of a total age cohort of over 650,000 children.[16]

Another cause has been the mixed reputation of many vocational awards and indeed over-frequent changes to the awards themselves. For example, CTCs introduced the BTEC diplomas into their schools, being the first schools to do so, and these proved very popular. Eventually these were replaced by the General National Vocational Qualifications and then vocational GCSEs in particular subjects, which were given the equivalence of four GCSE passes. The Labour government started to introduce diplomas as a new hybrid vocational and academic qualification. But the coalition has stopped funding them, and is seeking to develop its own rigorous alternatives, while discouraging schools from taking BTECs by reducing the tariff to a single GCSE, regardless of the size of the vocational qualification.

These constant changes, with the requirement for teachers to learn new syllabuses, have not been helpful. Unsurprisingly, few vocational awards achieve the high status of the 'gold standard' A-levels. It is also puzzling that proven awards, such as the City & Guilds diplomas in technical skills such as carpentry, plumbing and electricity, and more recently the Oracle and Cisco IT diplomas, have not been given the status they deserve. Both Cisco and headteachers have told me that an eighteen-year-old acquiring the Cisco Certified Network Associate Diploma after taking the 280-hour Cisco Academy introductory course, can walk straight into a £25,000 a year IT position, such is the shortage of IT workers.

Nationally, the situation has become needlessly confused. There are separate departments to cover pre-nineteen and post-nineteen education, with the Department for Education led by Michael Gove, who is responsible for schools and children's services, and the Department of Business Innovation and Skills, under Vince Cable, responsible for post-school education and skills, including universities. Further education colleges answer to both departments, and some training provision for young people, particularly apprenticeships, is the responsibility of BIS while full-time education of the same age group is a matter for DFE.

I think we could learn much from the successful system used in the Federal Republic of Germany, a country that I regularly visit. The European Centre for the Development of Vocational Training (CEDEFOP) published a fascinating study in 2007 of Vocational Education and Training in Germany.[17] Under article 20, the basic law (CG) of the German Constitution,[18] the sixteen *länder* or states which form the German Federal Republic are responsible for education. Each *land* is fundamentally responsible for education and culture. However, in order to ensure a minimum level of common factors, there is a standing conference of the *länder* Ministers of Education. While the *länder* are responsible for vocational training in schools, the federal government is responsible for in-company vocational training including apprenticeships.

The German economy is strongly export-oriented. In 2005, exports were equivalent to 35 per cent of GDP, while imports only accounted for 28 per cent. Because of the skills of its workers, Germany is the world's largest exporting nation ahead of the USA, China and Japan. In 2008, *The Economist* estimated that Germany achieved a trade surplus of $285 billion. This compares to the trade surplus of China of $253 billion and a deficit for Britain of $187 billion and the United States of $849 billion.[19] Germany's main exports include cars and car parts, machines, chemical and electrical products and foods.

A high proportion of students in Germany achieve an upper secondary school-level qualification. One reason for this is the long-standing institution of the dual system of vocational training in Germany. Sixty per cent of German sixteen- and seventeen-year-olds achieve an upper secondary school qualification, compared to only 42 per cent in the UK. There is a very high participation level of employers in the provision of education. Overall, 25 per cent of all German employers are currently providing training, with 91 per cent of the largest employers participating.

The German educational system starts in *kindergarten* for three- to six-year-olds. Children then transfer to primary school, where they remain until age ten. At age ten, pupils choose, with the advice of the parents and guidance from their teachers, to enter one of three different types of secondary school. Additionally, there are also comprehensive schools in almost all the *länder*.[20] There is no equivalent to the Eleven plus entry examination for English grammar schools.

The three different main types of schools are the primarily academic *gymnasium* attended by a third of German pupils, though a quarter of *gymnasium* students transfer to specialist grammar school (*fachgymnasium*) at the age of sixteen.[21] Intermediate Schools or *realschulen* educate another quarter of pupils. They are prepared for vocational qualifications as well as learning German, maths and science. Again, it is up to the children and their parents, with guidance from the teachers, whether they enrol in a *realschule* or *gymnasium*.[22] There are also a number of secondary general schools (*hauptschulen*), which are similar to British comprehensive schools, which 24 per cent of German children attend. There are also some comprehensive schools in almost all the *länder*.

A particularly interesting aspect of the German school system is that for all three types of secondary school, there is an orientation stage for two years. If a pupil is not performing well or enjoying their school, there is a provision for them to change to a different type of school at age twelve. At sixteen, students in *realschulen* and *hauptschulen* transfer to one of six vocational training options.

The dual system is by far the largest provider of education at upper secondary level. Of this age cohort, 53 per cent train for a particular occupation, such as engineering. After completing their training in the dual system, the majority of students take up employment as a skilled worker, but are encouraged to take additional qualifications. Of the vocational schools, the full-time vocational schools have the highest number of students. These schools prepare students for an occupation or for vocational training in the dual system.

The system is described as dual because training takes place in two places of learning – companies and vocational schools. The entrepreneurs bear the costs of the in-company training, and pay the trainees remuneration which averages about one third of the starting pay for a trained skilled worker.

At age eighteen, German students can choose to continue their education in either one of the 117 universities or one of the 164 *fachhochschulen*. Entitlement to study in *fachhochschulen* is provided by a certification confirming the academic standard required for entry (*fachhochschulreife*). Another important part of the German system is the provision of continuing vocational education, including preparation for higher diplomas in subjects such as engineering or construction skills.

Crucially, when I spoke to students in technical schools they regarded their schools as being as good as any other. They knew that those who had been before them had got great jobs, and that the vocational route was of equal if not higher status than university.

One significant reason for the British failure to train its sixteen- to eighteen-year-olds properly is over-prescriptive European Union health and safety and employment regulation. Unlike every other EU country, we have a Common Law structure which means that these rules are translated into British Law and are rigidly enforced. By contrast, the sixteen German *länder* have a constitutional court which gives every German *land* the right to opt out of EU rules they do not like. We need to change our relationship with the European Union so that we have the same powers to reject EU employment and health and safety rules as do the Germans.

But there is hope in Britain. Kenneth Baker's new university technical colleges are reviving the spirit of the old technical schools in a modern context, though there are still too few of them. I also strongly support the UTCs, but fear that because they are new schools for fourteen- to nineteen-year-olds, costing £8 million each, there will only be a few of them. As I argued earlier, a much better way to achieve high standards of technical education is to allow academies to offer high-quality technical education in addition to academic studies.

Why not, on an optional basis, allow academies, if they wish, to change their educational structure so that between the ages of eleven and fourteen all pupils would be taught by the same teachers, who would concentrate on the basics, especially literacy and numeracy? There would be two options at age fourteen, the first being a very high-quality technical option using City & Guilds diplomas and employing Oracle, Cisco and Microsoft academies to teach much-needed IT skills. At age eighteen the schools would arrange apprenticeships leading to further diplomas and hopefully employment. The second would be a high-quality academic option, preparing students for either the International Baccalaureate or A-levels, in order to gain entrance to university.

Practical steps to improve literacy and reduce unemployment would make a big difference. But we must also do more to harness peer pressure to motivate young offenders to live a more productive life. I was particularly impressed by a visit to the Delancey Street Foundation, based in San Francisco.[23] Founded by Dr Mimi Halper Silbert in 1971, this project taught 500 former offenders how to build their own apartment block and then start up a series of successful businesses including running a restaurant, a removals company, a car repair shop and many others.

Over the years, the Delancey Street Foundation has transformed the lives of 14,000 former offenders, and now operates in five US centres. Residents include teenagers and senior citizens, and men and women of all races and ethnicities. The average resident has been a hardcore drug and alcohol user, has been to prison, is functionally illiterate, and has a personal history of violence and poverty. Residents stay at least two years though most stay longer. During their time at Delancey Street, they are trained in three different marketable skills to enable them to return to the workplace. Beyond academic and vocational training, residents learn important values, and the social skills that will allow them to live successfully in the mainstream of society.

The San Francisco centre headed by Dr Silbert does not employ professional staff, but relies upon the social pressure to behave and work hard expected by the older members. For example, Dr Silbert re-frames the habit of reporting violations to the authorities as a vital behaviour, even a mission, that carries with it profoundly moral meaning. The centre says, 'This is our family and this is our home and in our home this is what we believe in. We develop a community based on simple moral ideas and then make the norms so strong that our community sustains them.'

As High Sheriff, I learnt a huge amount about the reasons why too many young people in our country turn to a life of crime. In my visits to schools and places like the Delancey Centre in San Francisco, I also learnt some of the solutions. While successive governments have sought to tackle youth crime, unemployment and illiteracy, there are still too many young people blighted by those three evils. I hope that we have the courage to take the radical steps needed to give these young people the hope and opportunities that could turn their lives in very different directions.

13

LESSONS IN LEADERSHIP

Reflections on Good Leadership, Examples of Successful Headteachers & Turning Around Failing Schools

My own experience of leading organisations, including AIFS and the CTC Trust, gave me new insights into the art of leadership. Of course, I had gained much of the theory at Harvard and seen it in action at Procter & Gamble. But there is nothing like real experience to put the theory into practice. One way I have learned a lot more about leadership is from meeting great headteachers and principals.

In many ways, England now has a lot to teach others about school leadership, and its quality has been praised by the Organisation for Economic Co-operation and Development (OECD) as being among the best of the world. I think that the leadership and innovation shown by leaders of CTCs, academies and specialist schools played a big part in transforming the status and expectations of school leadership, and I reflected on some of this when I was invited to give a lecture to the Federation of School Leadership in 2006 on how to turn around a failing school.

At that stage, I noted that there were 512 secondary schools in England – nearly one fifth of the total – where fewer than a quarter of their pupils obtained five good GCSE grades – defined as a C grade or higher – including in the core subjects of English and Maths. There were 400,000 children attending these schools. Many of their pupils would leave school at sixteen without the skills necessary to get a good job. There has been some improvement since and the coalition has set more demanding floor targets as a result.

There were many reasons why these schools underperformed. They were usually situated in areas of high social disadvantage with a high proportion of pupils eligible for free school meals. They had high concentrations of children of recent immigrants, many of whom did not speak English at home. Because the schools are unpopular they frequently have an unfair proportion of excluded children sent to them by other schools. But in most cases the principal problem with these schools was poor leadership, including weak headteachers and heads of departments, and ineffective governing bodies. My argument was that if we were to avoid continuing with such a two-tier system of education, we would need to recruit better leaders for these under-performing schools.

A National Audit Office report in 2005 said that there were 1,500 English primary and secondary schools which lacked a permanent headteacher. This represented a quarter of all primary schools and a fifth of secondary schools. One of the solutions I proposed to increase the stock of good headteachers was to encourage the setting up of more partnerships between high-performing schools and under-performing schools. Such partnerships are now increasingly common as more schools become academies, and with the growth of academy chains, trusts and federations.

While there was general agreement that we needed more good headteachers, there was still no general agreement on what made a good school. This often made the training of new headteachers ineffective. It was vital that aspiring young headteachers acquire the necessary skills to improve school performance.

One of the speeches at the conference was by Peter Rudd, the Principal Research Officer at the National Foundation for Educational Research (NFER). Together with several of his colleagues, he co-authored in 2002 an important study called 'High-performing specialist schools: what makes the difference'. From Peter's study, we learned that there are a number of common characteristics of high-performing schools:

A good leadership team of the headteacher, heads of department and governing body;

Their ability to attract and retain good teachers;

A focus on the basics such as literacy and numeracy;

The setting of targets and use of data to monitor progress;

Discipline and order;

Curriculum innovation, which may include vocational awards and/or the International Baccalaureate;

Extensive use of information communications technology (ICT) including linked wireless laptops and whiteboards;

Consideration of a longer school day and non-traditional term dates;

A focus on individual learning to create an ethos of achievement for all;

The support of parents and the use of older students as mentors.

There is probably still general agreement around those characteristics. But what makes a good leader, especially a good headteacher? A crucial characteristic of the good leader is the ability to develop a vision of what they wish to achieve and to persuade staff to support that vision by working together as a team. But I am particularly taken by the ideas of Jeffrey J. Fox, the American author and marketing consultant. One of his best-sellers provides a 'simple success formula' for a great boss.[24] He suggests ten key characteristics that could as easily be applied to headteachers:

Only hire top-notch, excellent people.
Put the right people in the right job. Weed out the wrong people.
Tell the people what needs to be done.
Tell the people why it is needed.
Leave the job up to the people you've chosen to do it.
Train the people.
Listen to the people.
Remove frustration and barriers that fetter the people.
Inspect progress.
Say 'thank you' publicly and privately.

Another of my favourite American authors on good leadership is Jim Collins, author of *Good to Great*. Collins emphasises the crucial role of a good leader in attracting to his or her organisation the very best people. He says the principal role of leaders is to 'get the right people on the bus; the wrong people off the bus, and the right people in the right seats'. Collins emphasises another important quality of leadership – the use of quantitative data to track progress.

I cited Fox and Collins to make my point, but I also argued that it was unfair to compare the examination performance of schools purely on the basis of raw results. I am a great believer in the importance of having clear goals for schools, and they have always been an essential part of the improvement drive in specialist schools and academies. But it is important that such comparisons are fair.

I think that value added comparisons, such as those developed by Professor Jesson for the SSAT, are the fairest way to compare the relative performance of schools. Jesson compares the average performance of eleven-year-olds, based on national tests, with the likely performance of pupils in their GCSEs five years later. Using point scores, this allows us to see how well a school is really doing given its intake. Good schools do better than their predicted achievement level and therefore add value. A school which achieves less than its predicted score is under-performing. Jesson has used this method to assess which selective grammar schools – where they all gain five good GCSEs – are doing most to add value.

But it can be difficult to find sufficient outstanding headteachers for every under-performing school, and this is where collaboration and cooperation between schools can be crucial in raising performance in weak schools. Such co-operation started with the changes that David Blunkett made to the specialist schools programme, which saw schools working together in sports or language partnerships, and expanded as federations, trusts and academy chains in the new millennium.

Schools That Impressed Me

I gave the conference two case studies that had particularly impressed me at the time. The first was the Ninestiles Federation in Birmingham, led by Sir Dexter Hutt, which was one of the first to develop the collaborative model that is now much more common. The federation began in February 2001 with Ninestiles School taking on responsibility of the improvement of Waverley School, then on the brink of being failed by the school inspectorate Ofsted and placed into 'special measures'. An initial eighteen-month contract was later extended for a further three years until August 2005. During this period, Waverley saw the proportion of pupils gaining five good GCSE grades rise from 16 to 75 per cent. Waverley was the most improved school in Birmingham in 2003 and the third-most-improved nationally in 2005. In 2003, The International School (then on the brink of failing its Ofsted inspection) also joined the federation on a three-year contract. It saw improvements from nine to 51 per cent between 2003 and 2005.

Ninestiles, as the lead school, also saw improvements, which is an important feature of successful partnerships, as it is necessary to reassure parents, teachers and governors in the lead school that their own progress is enhanced rather than impeded by helping partner schools. Of course, some of those improvements reflected a decision to use vocational qualifications to encourage rapid change. This has become much more controversial in recent years, as the coalition's Education Secretary Michael Gove has reduced their tariff in the league tables and placed greater emphasis on certain academic subjects. While academic subjects are undoubtedly important, we do need to strike the right balance. Strong vocational options are important from the age of fourteen, as in other countries. But it can also be useful for schools that need rapid improvement to show pupils that they can achieve qualifications as a way to encourage them to gain good grades in English and Maths. In any case, the improvements at Ninestiles have been sustained.

Ninestiles is now an academy, led by Christine Quinn, Sir Dexter's deputy, having converted in 2012, and Ofsted said in its most recent report on the school in 2009,

> this outstanding school has made many changes in order to fully meet the needs of all students and overcome any barriers to learning. Students' achievement is outstanding. Many students study sixth form courses early and leave school with an outstandingly wide set of academic and vocational qualifications. The proportion of students gaining five higher grade GCSEs is well above average.

Sir Dexter, a quite remarkable school leader, continued his work through Ninestiles Plus, and retired last year after having helped turn around three schools in Hastings, Sussex with his collaborative approach. He has three key pieces of advice for those setting up federations which he developed from his work at Ninestiles ten years ago, but which hold true today.

First, federations should increase the leadership capacity and enable more risks to be taken. Second, they should also enable the resources of the lead school to be deployed to support the partner school – for this to be meaningful, the lead school has to build in additional capacity, so that teachers are available to work intensively with teachers in the partner school. This can mean employing and paying for extra staff at the lead school. And finally, he says that an executive headteacher – who leads the federation – should not try to be the head of more than one school; it is a complete nonsense to regard the head of the partner school as a 'site manager'. The head of the partner school has to have above-average headship skills to lead and manage the rapid changes that are necessary for school improvement. In Dexter's case, as the federation expanded, he could not do justice to both the role of head of Ninestiles and meet federation commitments, so each Ninestiles Plus school has its own headteacher and Dexter has overall responsibility for the progress of all schools in the federation. One of his personal criteria for success is not to be regarded as 'head' of any one of the schools. His 'co-construct' strategy with the head of each school and the federation is only justified if each school makes more rapid progress than would otherwise be the case.

Dexter believed that groups of schools should be encouraged to form federations. There is now a real energy behind that idea in schools generally. He argued that federations characterised by line-management accountability between executive head and head could do this, but there was a great deal of confusion about this relationship. Many found it hard to think past the traditional stand-alone role of the head that they are familiar with. This led them to assume that the head within a federation could be a proper head, but more of a site manager, with the implicit assumption that the executive head must be a 'super head' and the 'real' head of all the schools within the federation.

Dexter believed that anyone who had tried this site manager model soon realised its limitations, but the notion is one that many find hard to lose. Perhaps we ought to pay more attention to the Royal Navy, where no one would question that each ship within a fleet has to have its own captain. At the same time, the fleet is line-managed not by a 'super captain', but in this case, by an admiral. This does not diminish each captain, but it does result in an organisational structure that facilitates collaboration and results in powerful progress. Its organisational structure underpinned Britain's naval success in the nineteenth century. The hard federation is its educational equivalent. Might it help us achieve educational success in the twenty-first century?

The benefits of the hard federation model – where schools are formally bound to the federation, unlike 'soft' federations where they can easily leave or fail to participate – are not just at leadership level, but also at teacher, parent, learner and system level. But there were some initial problems with the hard federation model, which were overcome when the 2006 Education Act made it easier to federate and actively encouraged schools to join formal federal trusts. Today, the government particularly encourages outstanding academies to work formally with weaker schools and is promoting trusts and federations to improve standards and achieve greater efficiencies, particularly in the primary sector.

The second case study that I discussed described how such a structure, in one short year, transformed the previously failing Mallory School in Lewisham. In September 2005, the school became part of a joint academy with the highly successful Haberdashers' Aske's City Technology College in Hatcham, with the previous failing school taking a new name: the Knights Academy. The Haberdashers set up a new trust to supervise the two schools. It has since added a primary school to the trust. The outstanding CTC headteacher, Dr Elizabeth Sidwell, was appointed chief executive of the two schools with individual headteachers being appointed to each school. Dr Sidwell has since been appointed by Michael Gove to be the Department for Education's

Schools Commissioner. The deputy head of the CTC became the head of the new Knights Academy, a post now held by the very able Andrew Day.

All of Mallory's existing pupils transferred to the new Knights Academy, as did most of the staff. The Haberdashers leadership made it a deliberate goal of its new partnership to replicate the successful Haberdashers' focus on stretching pupils to the maximum of their potential in the new school. Funding was made available for all of the pupils to acquire the smart navy-blue blazer, white shirts and ties of the Haberdashers Hatcham Academy. When I visited the school in July 2006, I was stunned that so many characteristics of a good school had been achieved in such a short time: order and discipline with a high level of attendance; the school opens at 7.30 a.m., with breakfast available, and stays open until 6 p.m.; there is a very good programme of extracurricular activities in the afternoon including sports; there is a huge emphasis on acquiring literacy and numeracy skills.

The proportion of pupils gaining five good GCSE grades increased from 15 per cent in 2004[25] to 29 per cent in 2006 (though it was still only 14 per cent including English and Maths); in the last year of the previous school there were almost no first-choice preferences for the school. Today, the school is thriving. In 2011, 57 per cent of pupils achieved five good GCSEs including English and Maths, with 31 per cent of pupils on the rolls in receipt of free school meals, well above the national average. The academy does well for pupils of all abilities, but it has particularly strong value added for those who performed poorly in the tests at eleven. Attendance has improved from around 60 to 94 per cent. This is a remarkable achievement which is being replicated by several other former CTCs working with other local schools, often as academies.

Many of today's academies have formed federations. The seventeen Harris academies under the brilliant leadership of Sir Daniel Moynihan have dramatically raised their standards. However, they use techniques such as fair banding to ensure their schools remain community schools. These collaborative examples were early pioneers of a school-to-school improvement model that it now at the heart of the education system. The SSAT that I chaired – under its various titles – played a remarkable role in helping advance the model and develop the idea of executive leadership. As a charity that drew on its members, it was often ahead of policy makers in spotting and advancing trends.

14
THE STORY OF LEXHAM GARDENS[26]

Revitalising a Victorian Square in London

As a child, I had enjoyed gardens, especially growing vegetables. I grew vegetables when I was in the Congo as a toddler, hindered by the occasional wild boar, and enjoyed having the same opportunities after returning to Yorkshire during the war. So I always had green fingers. But it was to be many years before I had another opportunity to revisit my childhood enthusiasm.

When we moved from Greenwich, Connecticut in 1970 to live at Lexham Walk in Kensington, which is still my UK home, Lexham Gardens was a run-down garden square. Access was restricted to the 230 residents who overlooked the square and paid the garden rate for its upkeep. Its rules were closely defined by the Kensington Improvement Act of 1851 which arose from the development of the Kensington area following the successful Great Exhibition in Hyde Park. The 1851 exhibition had attracted 6 million people and raised a profit worth £16 million at today's prices, enough to found the Victoria and Albert Museum and the Natural History Museum. Its legacy lies also in the garden squares of Kensington.

During the first twenty years that Judy and I lived at Lexham Gardens, we rarely visited the garden. It was poorly maintained, being essentially a stretch of uninviting grass with a nasty wire fence which had replaced the original Victorian wrought-iron railing that had been torn down in the war to provide metal for guns.

But in 1989, late one evening I was walking my beloved Pomeranian dog Benji around the square when I was astonished to see a For Sale notice board in the garden. The notice said that the freehold of the garden square would be sold by auction at a forthcoming sale to be held at the Berkeley Hotel, Knightsbridge. I had always assumed that the 230 garden ratepayers, including myself, who paid the modest garden rate to the council, owned the garden.

The Lexham Gardens Garden Committee was not very active at the time. When I suggested we try to raise the money necessary to buy the freehold of the garden ourselves, there was little response. I tried to raise money by calling residents, but had no luck. So, I then hired an estate agents adviser. He said that several big property companies were representing companies who wanted to buy the Lexham Gardens freehold in order to build an underground car park under the gardens, as well as new apartment blocks. This would, of course, have ruined the quiet tranquillity of the square.

I decided to go to the auction at the Berkeley Hotel myself, along with my new adviser. We were astonished to see so many prospective buyers, mostly property developers. Bidding was aggressive, but I felt compelled to give as good as I got, and the word soon spread that I represented the local residents.

After half an hour of frantic bidding, I succeeded in purchasing the site, which is just under an acre in size, for just £71,000. Returning home as the proud owner of a London garden square, I asked Judy what I should do next. Naturally, she said we should redesign and replant the garden. She obtained the name of a garden designer called Wilf Simms, who suggested completely redesigning the garden. This was no easy task with so many plane trees planted by the Victorians.

Instead of one boring, long, narrow, poorly maintained lawn, he suggested dividing the square into five different areas or 'rooms': This would include a social area – with paving stones, a gazebo, a small lawn, two ponds with fountains connected by a wooden bridge, and several border beds. There would be a quiet, medium-size lawn area for reading, equipped with benches and a shrubbery with beautiful flowering bushes. The centrepiece would be a large lawn with a flowerbed, on which Judy would place a huge statue of a horse, which she had originally given to our daughter Kirsten in New York, but which didn't fit well in her apartment.

There would be a circular rose garden at the far end of the garden with a walk around it. Instead of narrow paths following the fence on both sides of the garden, which accentuated the narrowness of the garden, the designer suggested installing a winding Breedon path (a type of sandy path material) on just one side of the garden. This had the extraordinary effect of making the garden seem much wider than it was. Subsequently we added a sixth area, which is a children's play area with swings, a slide and a climbing-frame.

The garden designer also suggested replacing the nasty wire fence with a beautiful replica of the original Victorian wrought iron railings with a gate at each end of the garden as well as installing six watering taps. There was endless debate on the garden committee on the plan, but I finally convinced them of the beauty of the new design. All this sounded great and would clearly look so much more attractive than what it would replace.

But who was to pay for the work? The garden committee had no funds and did not want to raise the garden rate by too much. So, I negotiated a loan from Kensington and Chelsea Council repayable over ten years for the £125,000 cost of the new railings. I paid any remaining costs from my own pocket. This was not an entirely philanthropic gesture on my part, and I regard this investment as one of the best things I have ever done in my life. Besides transforming the neighbourhood, it has given me endless pleasure. As a keen gardener, I like nothing better than working in the garden on weekends.

In the new garden's first summer in 1991, we were awarded the first prize in the All London Garden Squares Competition – competing against entries from 100 squares – as well as the first prize in the Brighter Kensington and Chelsea Garden Squares Competition. I was also awarded the Franklin Moore Cup of Gilt Metal special award by the London Garden Square Society.

A particular highlight was when the Queen Mother honoured us with a visit in 1996. When she arrived she was accompanied by all the Royal Parks gardeners, who wanted to see a good example of how a public square could be maintained. I was still High Sheriff at this stage, and I met her at the gate dressed in my uniform. We had been advised that she liked a particular type of sherry, which we made sure was available. As I was showing her the rose garden, she noticed the life-size horse that we had installed in the garden. Judy had bought this metallic statue for our daughter in New York, but it was far too big for her apartment, so we gave it a new home in Lexham Gardens. She was a delightful guest, and she stayed for an hour chatting amiably about the garden, well beyond the allotted fifteen minutes for which her visit had been scheduled.

The beautiful new garden has undoubtedly improved the quality of life in our square. From being largely occupied by bedsits, it has become a place of families with children who are delighted to have somewhere they can play safely so near to their homes. The experience has also breathed new life into the local residents' committee, which now plays an active role in ensuring that everyone acts like good neighbours, including by putting rubbish out on the right day.

Because we wanted to ensure that the new amenity is very much for those of us living in the square, the Garden Committee continues to limit access to local residents living in residences overlooking the square and who pay the garden rate as defined in the 1851 Kensington Improvement Act. The gates are locked and only residents hold keys. This gives further reassurance to parents about their children's safety and helps to ensure that the square never degenerates into what it had become in the seventies. In order to prevent unauthorised entry by individuals climbing the fence to either party or even sleep in the garden, the police advised us to install a number of garden lights, both free standing and on the trees, which automatically switch on at night. This has solved the problem. My solicitor, Clifford Joseph, prepared new and strict garden rules which were approved by a High Court judge and became part of the garden's statutory basis.

Many of the gardens in Kensington and Chelsea are fortunate in having been established under the 1851 Kensington Improvement Act. This means that the local council collects the garden rate for them. The annual cost of maintaining our garden is £33,000 which results in a modest garden rate for residents averaging just under £150 per family. For such a wonderful amenity, this seems a small price to pay, and we have been fortunate in employing, on a part-time basis, a succession of wonderful gardeners such as Oliver Dickinson, who currently holds the post. They have maintained the garden to a very high standard, resulting in our winning garden square prizes every year. One of their particular skills has been the nurturing and maintenance of beautiful lawns through feeding and watering – we have six watering pipes in the garden.

Every year when our garden square is open to the public along with the other London garden squares, we hold a garden party which the mayor, the Leader of the Council and the local MP usually attend. We have a children's entertainer and a jazz band with about 300 guests attending the open day in the first week of June.

Finally, in order to protect the beauty of Lexham Gardens, I have bequeathed the freehold of the gardens to my charitable trust upon my death with specific instructions that trustees will ensure no development of the ground below the gardens, such as a car park, will occur.

15

REFLECTIONS ON AMERICA
My Thoughts on Where the US Needs to Go Next

Lexham Gardens has been a great place to reflect on my life as I enter my seventy-seventh year. I think back on all my time in America and the changes I have seen since I first helped Miles Halford organise his charter plane in 1957.

I have retained a lifelong interest in all things American. So, over half a century after I enrolled at Harvard, I was invited to give a speech to the Oxford University International Relations Society on the subject of 'The United States of America: Has She Lost Her Power?' I've lived, studied and worked in America, established a thriving transatlantic business and have a wonderful American wife and daughter. I am proud of my Anglo-American background. It is with that background that I view its challenges and its continuing strengths.

The USA is still the most powerful and influential country in the world. The annual Gross National Product is over $15 trillion, twice that of China and four times that of Germany. It is only slightly less than the GNP of all twenty-seven EU countries combined. America has the advantage too that, for all the power of lobbyists, it is still a democratic country with a strong rule of law and comparatively low levels of corruption. It has huge control over great global institutions such as the World Bank and the United Nations, both of which are located in New York. And its military power is still unsurpassed.

Could the United States exercise this power for greater good in the world and are there serious domestic issues which need to be addressed? The answer to both questions is undoubtedly yes. Since Bill Clinton left office in 2001, his successors George Bush and Barack Obama have been less successful at addressing major domestic issues. Partisanship in Congress has not been overcome by a strong-willed White House, particularly in education, despite the efforts of the No

Child Left Behind programme and an energetic Arne Duncan, who improved Chicago schools, as Obama's Education Secretary.

At the Renaissance Conference in Santa Monica, California in 2012, I was invited to give hypothetical advice to President Obama. I focused on education, since I believe the Achilles' heel of the United States is the poor state of many of its state schools, especially in urban areas. Take just one example. New York City Schools District has a budget of $24 billion for just 1.1 million children – that's $21,800 per child. Yet over a third of their students fail to graduate from high school. Despite Mayor Bloomberg's recent reforms – which have improved the graduation rate – too many leave school at sixteen or seventeen without being able to read. There are many reasons for this, but the most serious is that it has until recently been virtually impossible to sack an incompetent teacher.

The world's greatest nation should not allow this to continue, with almost a quarter of its children dropping out of high school before graduation. In his second term, Obama needs to put more energy into the drive to improve state-funded schools, especially in urban areas, and he needs to halt the power of the teaching unions to impede progress. Outside some independently managed charter schools, the unions still dominate the administration of too many publicly funded schools, many of which are too small to attract strong managers. Teachers' contracts must be changed so incompetent teachers can lose their jobs.

Bill Gates, whom I met at a Harvard Business School alumni meeting, said in his speech that it would be very difficult to introduce effective national accountability standards in US schools because the Democrats, who are greatly influenced by the teaching unions, are against accountability and the Republicans, who tends to support states' rights, are against national policies on principle. I hope that in this case Bill is wrong.

Every child entering secondary school at the age of thirteen should be given a reading test. Those who are unable to read should be given special support. If you can't read, you can't learn. Practical national accountability standards must be introduced which cannot be circumvented by state education authorities, as happened with No Child Left Behind. And charter schools, particularly those with rigorous and proven programmes like Knowledge is Power (KIPP), should be supported, replacing failing schools with vigorous accountability standards. These schools should be encouraged to employ bright graduates as teachers.

I also believe that state-funded faith schools have an important role to play in US education. In England, they represent a third of all state-funded schools. But in the United States, people of faith must pay privately if they are not funded through scholarships. The Cleveland Supreme Court judgement should be approved, so that taxpayer funds can be given to parochial schools whose standards are generally higher than state schools.[27]

But while so many American urban schools leave much to be desired, American higher education, with its wide choice of institutions, is among the best in the world. Even so, it is a particular problem that American students are not being taught the skills in the STEM fields (Science, Technology, Engineering and Mathematics) which a successful modern economy which exports a significant proportion of its manufactured goods requires.

The United States also needs to improve its national financial status if it is to revive its economy. I am indebted to my friend Dan Rose in New York for some of his thoughts on this subject. The US national macro-numbers today are frightening. With a GDP of $15 trillion, US public debt to others is now $10 trillion and intergovernmental debt is over $4.5 trillion, with the total growing at the rate of $1.5 trillion a year. The present value of existing US unfunded domestic entitlements is huge; common estimates put them at $66 trillion: $35 trillion for Medicaid, $23 trillion for Medicare and $8 trillion for Social Security.

Of 51 million private homes with mortgages, 15 million are worth less than their debt. Three million homes have been foreclosed since 2007; another 11 million are in arrears.[28] The US national unemployment rate remains over 8 per cent and millions of workers have given up looking for work, and many have lost any unemployment benefits. Student loans now total over $1 trillion, and the rising default numbers are ominous. Opinion polls universally show a public anxious and pessimistic, pleading for government's pragmatic compromise on vital issues at a time of rising partisanship.

The United States, like the United Kingdom and Germany, must also face the ramifications of an ageing and longer-living population. This has led to huge increases in government expenditure in pensions and healthcare not funded by increased taxation. The spiritual father of the Tea Party movement, Grover Norquist, may want government expenditure reduced to 'the size where he can drag it into the bathroom and drown it in the bathtub', but most Americans do not. They want good government services which must be paid for by taxation. Edmund Burke, the father of modern conservatism, put it succinctly – 'to tax and to please is not given to men'. Europe has found that value added taxes, although regressive, are the least objectionable way to raise revenue, but American sales taxes are instruments of the cities and states. America must reduce its government expenditures and increase its revenues.

As Dan says, few observers would disagree that free market economies are more productive than rigidly controlled ones – leading to what Winston Churchill called 'the unequal sharing of blessings *versus* the equal sharing of miseries'. Few would disagree that to achieve optimum productivity and socio-economic stability, free market economies require some degree of government regulation. What that degree should be is 'the question'.

John Maynard Keynes' 'interventionist' followers and Friedrich von Hayek's 'hands off' supporters will always battle, but neither Keynes nor Hayek approved of swollen government, and both agreed that over-indebtedness leads to financial nightmares. Short-term 'stimulus' (preferably on desirable repairs to the deteriorating and inadequate US infrastructure) to provide immediate employment, and longer-term 'austerity' (with renewed savings and investment for continuous growth) reflect the best thinking of both. The $2 trillion which respected engineers have told the US President must be spent on infrastructure – for repairs, upgrades and expansions – will provide short-term jobs and long-term economic and social benefits. Had the US created an infrastructure bank (with an accelerated review process) three years ago, the results would already be apparent. Short-term fears of deflation, long-term fears of inflation and recurring fears of stagflation must be dealt with realistically and prudently.

A healthy economy requires a sensible balance between consumption and saving or investment. In America today, consumption is tilted in favour of private consumer goods and against public goods such as airports, parks, highways, or mass transit. The US financial services industry, like our own in the UK, whose function should be to 'oil the wheels' of society and to channel savings into productive enterprise, has become a world of its own, skimming a disproportionate share of the national income. In 2008, for example, the country's top twenty-five hedge fund managers personally received $25 billion among them, largely through the legal scam of low-tax 'carried interest'; and corporate CEOs receive huge bonuses even as their companies post major losses. No wonder the American 'best and brightest' are seduced by financial paper-shuffling rather than careers in the productive world. Eventually, even the investment world will realise that a smaller share of a growing economy is better for them than a larger share of a stagnant one.

National wealth cannot be distributed (or redistributed) until it is produced. The US, and indeed the UK, must focus as much on wealth production as well as on its division. Albert Einstein noted that 'in the real world, there are neither rewards nor punishments – only consequences'. The Americans must act so that the consequences of their actions take them where they want to go.

America needs to renew its manufacturing industry as much as Britain does. As in Britain, Americans cannot all work either for the government or for banks and other financial institutions. Americans need to make things too. US economic problems are remediable – but not in the immediate future. America is a resilient society and it will muddle through, but it must modify its expectations for the short term and again think long-term. As Adam Smith wrote, 'There is a lot of ruin in a country.'

However, the US has great strengths. To regain their national momentum – to refute those who speak of 'American decline' – it must act vigorously and wisely. Four specific areas cry out for effective US governmental action: improving public school education; improving US infrastructure such as roads and railways; improving foreign trade, and improving industrial policy. It is also important that America lowers the cost of political campaigning (by some form of public financing, or free access to TV) and tightens – not loosens – the regulation of political contributions (thereby lessening the influence of lobbyists) and ends political gerrymandering. Undue influence – whether of 'fat cats' like the Koch brothers or the Forbeses, or of labour leaders like Randy Weingarten – must be reduced. The recent Supreme Court decision allowing special interests to spend unlimited amounts backing favoured candidates needs legislative reversal. Political term limits and specific steps to increase transparency and accountability to voters should follow. In the meantime, we need more politicians like Teddy Roosevelt, of whom the 'bosses' complained, 'We bought him but he didn't stay bought!'

I think that with the right foreign policy the United States can do more to promote peace and understanding than has been the result of some of the decisions of George W. Bush. The US saved the world from Communism and Soviet dictatorship. However, its foreign policy since the millennium has left much to be desired. I strongly believe that Bush should have never invaded Iraq, which cost $1 trillion and which directly led to the deaths of over 100,000 civilians. A similar error occurred in invading Afghanistan – nobody in history has ever won a victory there.

I firmly believe that a much more sensible Middle Eastern policy needs to be created, which does not kowtow to the Israeli lobby. There are 2 billion Muslims in the world, out of a total world population of 7 billion. There are only 1 billion Christians, many of whom do not go to church. Better education for people in the Middle East and Pakistan is the key to improving the troubled political leadership there. The United States, with the help of Europe and indeed China and Russia, needs to learn more about what motivates fanatic Muslims and what measures would reduce their influence. The liberation of Libya was an excellent example of what co-operation can achieve.

The United States of America has been a huge part of my life for over half a century. I have watched it change in many ways. But it retains the can-do spirit that always attracted me, and from which we have so much still to learn. I hope that whoever leads that great country does so with a wisdom and understanding that we so need in today's world.

16

LESSONS FROM MY LIFE

Some Final Reflections on What I Have Learned

I may be seventy-seven but I am still active. I could retire easily but I like to stay engaged in my life's work. So I am still actively involved with the American Institute for Foreign Study as its chairman. I serve as chancellor of Richmond, the American International University in London and until recently I was a trustee of the Specialist Schools and Academies Trust. I also serve as chair of the British Friends of Harvard Business School and the Lexham Gardens Residents Association.

I strongly believe that the brain, like any other muscle, needs constant exercise. If one is physically fit, one should keep working. In reviewing my life through writing this book, I think I have learnt a little about the principles that underpin a successful life and career.

Education has been at the heart of much of my life. But I would not have been able to achieve as much as I did without having had a good education myself, and some great teachers and mentors along the way. I was fortunate to attend a good secondary school. Without the support of Dr Thomas Kingston Derry at St Marylebone Grammar School, London, I would never have gained entry to Cambridge University or to Harvard Business School. And, at Cambridge, the wise advice of Dr Runcie helped me to make the right choices about Harvard.

No leader can work without a good team. You can't do everything yourself and you need to have only the best and most able people working for you. AIFS is doing well because it has superb leadership in Bill Gertz, Jack Burg, Mike DiMauro, Peter Jones and Becky Tabaczynski in the US with every one of its eight divisions having a good director, and similarly superb leadership in London with Mike Berry, Ailsa Brookes, Mark Simpson, Janet Henniker-Talle and Linda James and with Thomas Kiechle, who leads our German subsidiaries.

Richmond is doing very well under the leadership of its new president, Dr John Annette.

I could not be effective myself in my endeavours without the wonderful support and strong management given to me by Debbie Wilson, who has worked at AIFS for nearly a quarter of a century as the head of my private office, and Hannelore Fuller, who has worked for me for six years as my PA and diary manager.

In our reform of failing British schools through conversion to academies, the crucial element in turning round a failing school is appointing a good headteacher who then recruits the right leadership team and teachers. The corollary of course is that if you have made the wrong appointment, and you have someone who is incompetent, it is important to rectify that mistake as quickly as possible.

I have benefited greatly from learning and working in different cultures. I have written a lot about my transatlantic experiences in this book. But my cultural influences include my Congolese childhood, my time serving with the King's African Rifles in Kenya and the many countries I have visited over the years for work or pleasure.

I have always adhered to honest and respectable standards of behaviour in my business dealings. I don't believe there is any other way that you can do business and succeed in the long term. Of course, recent events have shaken the faith of many people in business and politics. But most politicians and business people are honest in their dealings, and our great political and financial leaders have always acted honestly and in the best interests of their constituents or shareholders. I have learned that business leaders and political leaders who always put their personal interests first will inevitably fail.

Both the world of business and politics are now multinational. I studied Latin and Greek and speak French, Italian, Swahili and some German. It is essential that young people learn other languages and understand the cultures of countries with whom they will be working. It allowed me to become an effective courier as a student, and an effective businessman in later life. Our future business success as a nation certainly requires improved linguistic and cultural understanding.

I think it is a real shame that the numbers learning languages have dropped in recent years. More British students should study abroad and learn another language. But they shouldn't just learn French or German, the languages most often taught in British schools. Our specialist language schools did a lot to encourage greater breadth in language learning. Crucial languages in the future will be Mandarin, Spanish and Arabic, and it is good that more English children are learning these languages. You cannot do effective business in China if you do not speak the language.

Physical fitness is crucial to a successful career. When I attended the fiftieth-year reunion of my class of 1961 in 2011 at Harvard Business School, I was shocked at the poor health of many of my classmates, and the number that had retired or died. Of course, I enjoy a glass of wine, but I know that more than a couple of glasses a day is bad for me. I don't smoke or take drugs. Most important of all is regular physical exercise. I swim on most days and walk to work, exercise my dog Lester and garden like a maniac. I have always regarded it as essential to get a decent night's sleep.

Good financial skills have been as important. Learning how to manage one's own personal financial affairs is crucial. I graduated from Harvard Business School with no money, having relied on a generous scholarship to fund my second year. But Harvard taught me a lot about finance. And I learned good business discipline at Procter & Gamble for four years, before founding AIFS, which is still flourishing nearly fifty years later. Roger Walther, my partner at AIFS, is a financial genius. He taught me how to judge a possible deal and the crucial importance of having good legal and tax advice. Having good financial advice is also crucial in preserving one's own financial resources. I don't like investing in leveraged hedge funds but prefer high-quality US common shares and bonds. One important lesson I learnt in the early days of AIFS was that it is important to develop good relations with your bank and to agree lines of credit when you or your company is doing well, not when you are in financial trouble.

I think it is important that schools should do more to teach financial and enterprise skills so that young people know how to manage their personal budgets and know how to start their own business. Once again, many specialist schools and academies helped pioneer such teaching in English schools, often with the help of sponsors.

I have enjoyed having the opportunity to do good in the world. Nothing gives one greater satisfaction than doing good things for others. As the founder and chairman of the Specialist Schools and Academies Trust (SSAT), I helped to substantially improve standards of education in 3,000 English schools. As chairman of AIFS, we have helped 1.5 million students from over 100 countries to learn each other's languages and to understand their cultures. Those young people are the reason why I continue to work and enjoy what I do so much. Seeing so many gain life-changing experiences through education or exchanges is a huge reward in itself.

For me, it has been important too to have other interests. A love of gardening turned itself into a drive to restore one of London's most beautiful garden squares, helping save Lexham Gardens from becoming a parking lot. It is now regarded as one of the most beautiful garden squares in London, having won the All London Garden Squares Competition six times as well as the Brighter Kensington and Chelsea Garden Square competition. But what gives me the greatest satisfaction is being able to enjoy its beauty whenever I can, whether sitting on a park bench or walking my dog, Lester.

But my greatest joy has been having a happy, stable and rewarding family life. In 2015 I will have been married for fifty years to the same lovely lady I met in Cincinnati and who gave me the idea to set up AIFS. Judy and I have a lovely daughter, Kirsten. Without their love and support, I would never have achieved all that I did.

NOTES

1. http://www.raf.mod.uk/history/campaign_diaries.cfm?diarymonth=9&diaryyear=1940&diaryday=18.

2. http://pentecostalpioneers.org/JamesSalter.html.

3. 2011 statistics: http://www.education.gov.uk/inthenews/inthenews/a00198585/looked-after-children-statistics-2011.

4. http://www.education.gov.uk/rsgateway/DB/SFR/s001046/sfr30-2011v3.pdf.

5. See 'A Better Education for Children in Care', Social Exclusion Unit, 2003.

6. The Institute of Economic Affairs published my paper on 'How English Universities Could Learn from the American Higher Education System' in 2009. This can be obtained from the IEA at www.iea.org.uk.

7. Leslie Chapman's *Your Disobedient Servant: the Continuing Story of Whitehall's Overspending* was published as a Penguin Special in 1979.

8. Readers interested in learning more of the GLC reforms between 1977 and 1981 which reduced the white-collar staff are invited to read my paper, 'The Elected Members Guide to Reducing Public Expenditure' published jointly by the Conservative Political Centre and the Bow Group in 1980.

9. A copy of a letter from John Major on the initiative is in the Appendix.

10. DCMS 2009 estimates for GVA.

11. *Daily Mail*, 26 May 2012.

12. Civitas crime fact-sheet on Youth Crime in England and Wales.

13. International Centre for Prison Studies statistics.

14. http://www.opsi.gov.uk/RevisedStatutes/Acts/ukpga/1944/cukpga_19440031_en_1.

15. Department for Children, Schools and Families: www.dcsf.gov.
uk/publications/furthereducationdocs.

16. DCSF Press Release 2007/0065.

17. 'Vocational Education and Training in Germany', *Cedefop Panorama*, 138 (Luxembourg Office for Official Publications of the European Community, 2007). Copies in English can be accessed at www.cedefop.europa.eu.

18. Bundesministerium fuer Bildung und Forschung.

19. *The Economist*, 27 September 2008, back page. http://www.
economist.com/

20. 'Vocational Education and Training in Germany', *Cedefop Panorama*, 138 (Luxembourg Office for Official Publications of the European Community, 2007) p. 22.

21. 'Grund- und Strukurdaten 2007/2008' (Bundesministerium fuer Bildung und Forschung) p. 25.

22. 'Vocational Education and Training in Germany', *Cedefop Panorama*, 138 (Luxembourg Office for Official Publications of the European Community, 2007).

23. http://www.delanceystreetfoundation.org/wwa.php.

24. Jeffrey J. Fox, *How to Become a Great Boss: Winning Rules for Getting and Keeping the Best Employees* (Vermillion, 2002: reprinted 2010).

25. No published figure is available including English and Maths for 2004.

26. This chapter is based on an article I wrote for the *Garden Square News* edited by Holly Smith, which was printed in the autumn of 2011 under the title 'A Tailor-Made Square'.

27. To learn more about these ideas, read my book *A Good School for Every Child* (David Fulton, 2009).

28. http://www.forbes.com/sites/morganbrennan/2012/02/09/how-the-25-billion-foreclosure-settlement-will-really-affect-the-housing-market/.

APPENDICES

1. AIFS Study Abroad for US college students – list of host universities throughout the world
2. Curriculum for the three-week Summer Institute for the Gifted programme at Princeton
3. Key events in the history of AIFS
4. Purchase agreement with the Methodist Church for the purchase of Richmond College by AIFS
5. Letter from Prime Minister Thatcher in 1990 supporting the launch of the Specialist Schools initiative
6. Letter from Prime Minister John Major in September 1993 congratulating Cyril Taylor on the successful launch of the specialist schools
7. List of Secretaries of State for Education for whom I served as special adviser.
8. List of GBE members
9. Copy of letter from Tony Blair congratulating Cyril Taylor on his work as chair of the Specialist Schools and Academies Trust
10. Copy of letter from Prime Minister Gordon Brown thanking Cyril Taylor for his work in improving standards in English schools
11. Brief for sponsors of specialist schools
12. Front cover of original AIFS brochure in 1964
13. Chart showing the basic structure of German secondary education
14. Fund-raising brochure of the British Friends of Harvard Business School
15. Presidents of Richmond, the American International University in London
16. Honorary degree recipients of Richmond, the American International University in London
17. Publications by Cyril Taylor
18. The American Institute for Foreign Study: ethos and divisions

Appendix 1: AIFS Study Abroad for US college students – list of host universities throughout the world

AIFS study abroad programmes are currently organised at the following institutions:

University of Belgrano, Buenos Aires, Argentina
Murdoch University, Perth, Australia
University of Salzburg, Austria
Fundação Armando Alvares Penteado, São Paulo, Brazil
Universidad Adulfur Ibanez, Vina del Mar Chile
Beijing Language and Culture University, China
Veritas University, Costa Rica
Charles University, Prague, Czech Republic
Richmond, the American International University in London, England
University of the South Pacific, Fiji
Collège International de Cannes, France
University of Grenoble, France
University of Paris IV (Sorbonne), France
Catholic University of Paris, Paris, France
American College of Greece, Athens, Greece
Humboldt University, Germany
University of Hyderabad, India
University of Limerick, Ireland
Richmond in Florence, Italy
Richmond in Rome, Italy
Victoria University of Wellington, New Zealand
Pontificia Universidad Católica Peru, Lima, Peru
St Petersburg State Polytechnic University, Russia
Stellenbosch University, South Africa
Universidad Autonoma, Barcelona
University of Granada, Spain
University of Salamanca, Spain
Bogazici University, Istanbul, Turkey

Appendix 2: Curriculum for the three-week Summer Institute for the Gifted programme at Princeton

Courses for Students Ages 10, 11, or 12 at Program Start
Humanities
Speaking, Writing, Empowering! (Jo1): Learn how to be a mass communicator through developing your writing and public speaking skills. Work on precision of language, imagery, figures of speech, and the revision process. Discover how you can use the power of your words to motivate, persuade, influence, inform, or entertain others. Investigate how to turn your skills, interests, and knowledge into speaking topics. Become a communicator who will have the potential to earn applause, admiration, and financial prosperity while motivating others.

The Past is Present: Anthropology in Action (Jo2): Have you ever wondered why rituals and traditions play such a big role in the world? Or what we can learn from excavating centuries-old structures? Anthropology is the study of humans, what we know, what we think about, and even what we still question. Anthropology studies behaviour and traditions of humans, both in the present day and in the past. Investigate a culture and determine what social and cultural influences lead to their current culture. Create a fictional culture and trace the group's path through the events of the last century. What do you think future anthropologists will find fascinating about the twenty-first century?

Going to Court (J03): 'All rise for the honourable judge... you!' Through the process of enacting trials, you will experience the justice system of the United States. You'll take on the roles of judge, jury, prosecutor, defender or witness. Through active involvement in the courtroom drama, you will learn to organise facts, develop your speaking and questioning abilities, and understand the concepts of justice through jury deliberation.

Fantasy Fiction Fun (J04): What would the world be like without Harry Potter and other fictional characters who make us love reading? Immerse yourself in the genre of fantasy fiction, explore and celebrate what makes it unique, then create your own fictional characters and the worlds in which they live. You could be the next J. K. Rowling!

Math and Science

Creative Math Paths (J05): Develop your math problem-solving ability as well as your real-life problem-solving strategies. Challenging problems will provide opportunities for intuitive and inductive reasoning, mathematical discovery, reasoning skill, insight, creativity, and originality. Expand your thinking through mathematical activities, and discover multiple methods to solving a problem. Construct and refute arguments using symbolic and numerical data. This course is great preparation for real-life problem solving.

Anticipating Algebra (J06): 'When will I ever use algebra?' you ask. Here's one way. Introduce yourself to pre-algebra through this class that focuses on applications of algebra in the world. In addition to tackling concepts of linear equations, polynomial functions and factoring, you may also have time for fun with games, tessellations, and probability.

The Need for Speed (J07): As a society we're moving faster than ever; the need for speed is pervasive in the transportation and communication industries. Investigate the science and mathematics of speed! Starting with speed in transportation, explore the physics of speed in air, land, and water by designing a route via land, sea and air to traverse the world as quickly as possible, with the opportunity to design a new, fast vehicle! Consider the need for speed in communication. How has the need for speed influenced technological innovations in cell phones, push-to-talk, texting and the internet? Evaluate the need for speed in cyberspace and digital communications networks. Do you feel the need for speed?

Chemistry

The Essential Element (J08): Welcome to the laboratory that is the world in which you live. Experiment with domestic chemicals, environmental materials, foods, and living organisms to discover the chemical nature of substances, their properties, reactions and uses in daily life. Design a series of experiments to test your hypotheses about the reaction of substances.

DNA: Your Unique Code (J09): How do cells make copies of themselves? How do your hair follicles generate protein to keep growing? The answers to these questions are DNA replication and protein synthesis. Investigate the structure of DNA and the processes by which it creates proteins. Learn what turns genes on and off. Gain an understanding of the structure that holds all the information and controls every cell within a living organism. Debate the ethical uses of DNA knowledge and the pros and cons of biotechnology.

Do You See What I See? (J10): Have you ever stared at an optical illusion for hours, just wondering how the image was created, and how your mind was tricked? Do you know why people see colours differently, and why some people and animals only see certain colours, or even only in black and white? Investigate what you can and can't see with your eyes, learn about the anatomy of the eye, and how glasses and contact lenses help to correct people's vision. Research eye colour and pigmentation, and the science behind albinism and heterochromia, having eyes of two different colours. Future optometrists and ophthalmologists, this class is for you!

Multi-Disciplinary

Cunning Camouflage (J11): In the animal world, the easiest way to avoid being eaten is to avoid being seen. There are innumerable examples in nature such as the chameleon, the zebra, and the stick insect. In the world of humans, camouflage has played an increasing role in the military. Camouflage is now popular in our modern culture as fine art and fashion. This course will examine how camouflage is used to hide and deceive in multiple contexts for various purposes. Students will design a new camouflage product and assess their need to stand out or be camouflaged' in their lives.

Sneaker Economics (J12): Do you own a pair of sneakers? Do you know anyone who doesn't? Did you know that an $80 pair of sneakers only has about $11 worth of materials in it? Sneakers and athletic shoes are a multi-billion-dollar industry and are so much a part of our lives that they provide a great way to learn about economics, technology and discovery, and innovation and design. In this class, students will explore the development of the athletic shoe over the last 100 years, while learning about the health and science of foot support as well as the economics and fashion aspects of the sneakers industry. Design the perfect sneaker for a niche market!

Spying: Secrets, Surveillance, and Science (J13): Did you know that the newest satellite technology can look into your living room from thousands of miles away in space? Have you ever wondered what it would be like to be a spy and monitor this technology? Did you know that some of the gadgets from James Bond really exist? Come discover how spies keep – or uncover – secrets. Get an inside look at the science behind the spy's tricks of the trade. Create an original spy gadget and persuade your peers of its usefulness.

Move Over Sherlock (J14): How do real detectives solve mysteries? Come examine how modern crime investigators use cutting-edge scientific discoveries to search for evidence, gather clues, and analyse data. Participate in a simulated mystery where you become the detective as you learn skills in logic, inductive and deductive reasoning, data collection, and analysis. This is a great way to practice using your scientific problem solving skills!

Research Methods: Informative Writing for Middle School and Beyond (J15): Learn the steps in writing effective research papers, starting with taking notes and creating detailed outlines. Discover the world of research methods outside of Internet search engines! Discover how to evaluate sources and how to cite and quote sources correctly. Pick an area of personal interest and write an original research paper using MLA or APA style.

Courses for Students Ages 13 or 14 at Program Start

Humanities

The Writer's Palette (M16): Learn how to create a masterpiece of characterization and setting. Gain experience and practice writing effectively and creatively by analysing and editing your own work. Discussions about style, the structure of fictional pieces, and reader involvement will help you understand the functions of writing as communication of knowledge as well as of creative expression.

Word Power (M17): Amaze your friends with your verbal prowess. Build a vibrant vocabulary and learn the secrets to deciphering new words. Explore the fascinating and often humorous world of word and phrase origins. Increase your verbal reasoning skills.

What's Your Point? (M18): Did you ever feel strongly about a controversial issue but felt unable to state your position? This debate course will help you do just that. You will have the opportunity to argue controversial issues using a debating format. The content will stress public speaking delivery, organizational skills, quick thinking, awareness of issues, and knowledge of current events. You will leave with a readiness for advanced forms of debate.

Roots of Human Behavior (M19): What are the theories behind why we act as we do? Study the psychology of human behaviour to help you understand more about yourself. This course will survey past and current theories in human development, mental health, and social relationships. You'll examine the roots of personality and behaviour as seen through the theories of Freud, Skinner, Maslow, and Erickson. You'll have a chance to evaluate the validity of the theories in the light of your own life experiences.

Immortality: Myths, Legends and the Supernatural (M20): Literature is replete with the search for the key to immortality. What drives the human fascination with never-ending life? Evaluate humankind's need for eternal life in literature, from vampire tales to the Greek Gods. Investigate historical quests for immortality, including the search to the Fountain of Youth and the alchemist's dream of the Philosopher's Stone. Create your own story of the quest for immortality.

Journey into Jurisprudence (M21): 'Hear ye, hear ye... the trial is about to begin.' Mock courtroom drama will unfold as you become the players in a series of exciting simulated trials that depict the way our legal system functions. The structure of our court system, the functions of judge and jury, basic trial procedures and the strategies that attorneys use to win cases will be explored. Develop your abilities to organize and interpret facts, to ask questions, and to make effective decisions.

Evolution of the Media (M22): Extra! Extra! Read all about it! The art of journalism has changed drastically since newsies sold papers on street corners. Evaluate the ethics of journalism, from early newspapers to modern internet news sites. Learn how to be a good consumer of news: who do you trust (and how do you know?). Predict the future directions of journalism. Create a newspaper during your three weeks at SIG.

Math and Science

Algebraic Expressions (M23): For those students who have not yet taken Algebra I, let us introduce you to linear and quadratic equations, polynomials, rational functions, and graphing. Class highlights include factoring algebraic expressions and using algebra in solving word problems. Please note: Pre-Algebra is an absolute prerequisite for this class!

Geometric Highlights (M24): For math lovers who have not yet studied geometry, here's a chance for you to explore this fascinating field of math.

Learn the secrets of the Golden Rectangle and the Divine Proportion. Investigate the power of symmetry. Topics may include the notion of proof, congruent triangles, perpendicularity, parallelism, geometric inequalities, similarity, circles and spheres, area and volume, and vectors. Pre-requisite: Algebra I.

Statistics: Methods in Data Analysis (M25): Investigate statistical concepts such as null, error, confidence and significance. Practice data analysis methods including regression, contingency tables and analysis of variance. Extend your new knowledge of statistical analysis by researching applied statistics in fields such as actuarial science, business, psychology, and engineering. Keep a handle on your fantasy baseball league by learning the statistical methods used to analyse games, players, and more!

Bonding with Chemistry (M26): Gain entry into the chemist's world by exploring some of the abstract concepts of chemistry that provide the basis for studying higher levels of this subject matter. You'll study topics such as chemical formulas, equations, stoichiometry, the chemistry of metals and nonmetals, chemical bonding, polarity, and acid-base chemistry.

Biology Basics (M27): Discover the secrets of the building blocks of life! Come get acquainted with some of the fundamental principles and processes of biological systems. You will be introduced to basic chemistry, metabolism, photosynthesis, cellular energy processes, reproduction and genetics. Gain insight into how living things coexist.

Engineering in Action (M28): Ever wonder how chemical, mechanical, electrical, aeronautical, and civil engineers solve real world problems? Come learn basic engineering principles surrounding stability of structures, buoyancy, heat phenomena, and electricity. Perhaps you will use your interest in scientific and mathematical principles to design towns, factories, airplanes, toys, and other products that will enhance your life in the future, or maybe you will pursue one of the many great career opportunities that abound in engineering!

Robot Rendezvous (M29): Did you know that robotics experts study the movement of insects and birds and mimic it in the movement of the robots they design? This class will explore machines, types of forces and structures, motion and performance analysis. You'll be a part of a team to simulate designs and constructions of robots that fulfil specialized functions. You will also engage in discussions about the future of robotics and the ethical considerations of their design.

Multi-Disciplinary

Analysing Aviation: Airfoils to Zeppelins: (M30): How is it that a 747 that can carry 600 people and can weigh 870,000 pounds at takeoff can lift itself into the air and fly up to 7,000 nautical miles without stopping? It is truly incredible when you think about it! This course will help you think about the science that makes flight possible, such as the forces of weight, lift, drag, and thrust. It will also look at the current status of the aviation industry. Students will design, construct, and test models and create a new design or solution to an aviation industry challenge. Come fly with us!

Thinking Outside and Beyond the Box (M31): In 1948, when George de Mestral made a connection between the burrs stuck to his pants and a way to fasten things together (which became Velcro), he was 'thinking outside the box'. Here's a class that will help you learn to do just that and perhaps come up with the next great idea! People who are able to make unique parallels and see new solutions will become our most valued problem-solvers of the future. Learn strategies and gain multiple perspectives that will assist you in applying creative solutions to problems now and in your future.

Beauty is in the Eye of the Beholder (M32): What is beauty? What facial features constitute physical beauty across cultures? What constitutes beauty in art and music and how has the perception of beauty changed over time? How does social networking impact the perception of beauty and the role of beauty in forming relationships? Discover beauty in all of its forms, from scientific research to artistic representation. Create a new model of beauty, using nature, art, science or humanity as a muse.

The Female Warrior (M33): In 2004, the 2,000 year-old remains of a female warrior buried with her sword were found in Iran. Despite the popular version of history that tells of how men conquered the world, there is evidence of strong, powerful female leaders throughout the world's history. Investigate female warriors from the Tru'ng sisters of Vietnam to Joan of Arc. Evaluate the characteristics of powerful female warriors and how these characteristics apply to modern women. Study the role of female leaders and evaluate the changing role of women in business, politics and the military. Create a prototype of the modern female warrior.

Theories of Time Travel: Spacetime Physics and Wormholes (M34): If we could unify quantum gravity, quantum mechanics, and general relativity into one theory, physicists argue that time travel would be possible. Journey with us through a study of black holes, negative energy, and cosmic strings as we research current theories of time travel. Study the experiments of physicists around the world and what they have revealed about paradoxes and mutable time lines. Create your own theory of time travel based on your research.

Satellite Science: Patrolling Planet Earth (M35): In 1957, the Soviet Union successfully launched Sputnik, the first artificial satellite, into space. In the 50 years since, satellites have evolved from sending simple radio transmissions to relaying complex images and data. The role of satellites has evolved from navigation and espionage to include weather tracking, television and telephone communication, and geopositioning. Investigate the burgeoning careers in satellites, from design and construction to interpretation. Learn how to interpret satellite data in an area of interest. Design a new satellite to solve a problem in everyday life.

Courses for Students Ages 15, 16, or 17 at Program Start
Humanities
Word Origins for SAT Success (S36): The etymology of words is a fascinating study in unlocking the complexities of linguistic relationships. This class will improve your vocabulary and understanding of word origins. You'll have the chance to practice taking sample tests, learn test-taking tactics, and improve your verbal confidence. You'll employ your new vocabulary as you practice writing for the current SAT writing component.

Writing Matters (S37): Do you want to move people with your words? This intensive workshop in exposure to the varied styles of contemporary authors and in developing your own writing style will challenge and motivate you. You'll gain invaluable practice in communicating your thoughts, feelings, and knowledge, vividly and expressively through the written word.

Guiding Principles of Philosophy (S38): Now, more than ever, the western and eastern parts of the world must strive to understand each other. Survey the major philosophical traditions of Eastern and Western civilization and analyse important social and political issues from various perspectives. Study some of the famous philosophers such as Lao-Tze, Confucius, Socrates, Plato, Hume, Kant, and Nietzsche. Develop a philosophy of your own.

Paradigm Shifts through History (S39): Who were the movers and shakers throughout time? Investigate the major shifts in the social, political and scientific world and the individuals instrumental in these paradigm shifts. Consider world-changing contributions in science, globalization, communications, religion and transportation. Predict the next shift and describe your future role in it!

Math and Science

Highlights of Algebra II (S40): Come hit the highlights of Algebra II and trigonometry, such as quadratic and cubic polynomials, the binomial theorem, the Principle of Mathematical Induction, irrational expressions, complex numbers, and exponential and logarithmic functions. A scientific calculator is recommended. (Prerequisite: Algebra I and Geometry)

Topics in Trigonometry (S41): Discover topics in trigonometry including the measurement of angles and radians, evaluating pi, the laws of cosines and sines, the Pythagorean theorem and rational and irrational numbers. A graphing calculator is recommended. (Prerequisite: Algebra I and Geometry)

Jump Start Your SAT Math Score (S42): Don't sweat those Math SATs; prepare for them. This class is designed to help you improve your math scores on standardized exams. Using past sample practice tests, you'll gain the confidence and skill you need to score well on standardized tests. Bring your scientific calculators. (Prerequisite: Algebra I and Geometry)

Physics in the News (S43): Understand the science behind the headlines! Investigate the scientific implications of important events happening across the world, including oil spills and earthquakes. Understand the physics behind the breakdown of the levy system in New Orleans and the Minnesota bridge collapse. Become an informed consumer of news, as you investigate the facts about nuclear power and get the full story behind global warming.

Applications of Chemistry (S44): This chemistry class will look at the theories and laws of chemistry. You will study stoichiometry, chemical periodicity, chemical bonding, organic chemistry, equilibrium, and redox reactions. A pocket calculator is required.

Medical Research: Is it in Your Future? (S45): As the baby boomers reach retirement age, opportunities in the field of medical research are expected to grow much faster than other occupations. There will be a great need for research related to the health issues associated with AIDS, cancer, Alzheimer's and antibiotic resistance. Discover the nature of this work, the typical working conditions, and the training qualifications to find out if this is the field for you. Research related fields such as pharmacology, microbiology, and infectious disease control. This course may direct you toward your future career.

The Science of Immortality (S46): The quest for immortality did not end with the search for the Fountain of Youth and the Philosopher's Stone. Study what exists beyond the myths; discover the science behind the search for never-ending life. Investigate both holistic and medicinal drugs that extend life. Critically examine plastic surgery as a tool for defying age. Research human cloning, cryonics, and cybernetics as methods of gaining eternal life and project the future of the field of immortal science.

Crime Scene Investigation (S47): Learn fingerprinting, hair analysis, handwriting analysis, and the importance of chain of custody when solving a crime. This introduction to forensic science will cover evidence collection guidelines, photography, profiling, and career training. Crime scene investigators draw upon their knowledge of chemistry, biology, physics, entomology, botany, and computer science to solve their mysteries. Investigate whether this could be a career for you. Create a mystery for your peers to solve.

Multi-Disciplinary

The Brain and Dreaming: To Sleep, Perchance to Dream (S48): Examine dreaming from physiological, psychological, and spiritual perspectives. Compare gender differences in dreams. Debate links between dreams and ontology. Gain an understanding of dream incorporation, lucid dreaming, and dreams of absent-minded transgression. Examine historical perspectives of dreams and their importance. Study the work of artist Salvador Dali and others who depict dreams in their art. Keep a dream journal with interpretations based on both Jungian and a Freudian point of view. Analyse the importance of dream interpretation in our present society.

SIG Apprentice (S49): If you have an interest in business and marketing, here's a chance to test and hone your skills. Teams of students will compete against each other in accomplishing increasingly challenging business and marketing tasks. After each task, students will enter the 'boardroom' for an assessment of their results and then take their new skills and ideas into the next assignment with a newly formed team. While no one will be 'fired', the competition will be tough! Great preparation for the real world!

College Preparation (S50): What you really need to know about the college application process from the test taking, to the essay, to the campus visit, to the interview. Learn how to write an essay that will impress the reader with its unity and coherence. Gain valuable test-taking strategies. Create a résumé that describes the real you. Practice interview questions and behaviours that will make a lasting impression. Gain the confidence to improve your chances for acceptance into the most highly regarded colleges.

Visual and Performing Arts Courses

Visual and performing arts courses are open to all ages, ten through seventeen, with the exception of Digital Photography which is limited to students who will be age thirteen–seventeen by the time the selected program starts.

Lock, Pop, and Hip Hop (A51): Bring your sneakers and your soul! It's all about having fun and feeling healthy. You'll learn the most up-to-date dance moves while you get a great aerobic workout! Learn body rolls, arm rolls, moon-walking and more! Experience imaginative choreography and improve your stage presence. Create a new dance form.

Script Writing, Page One, Re-Write! (A52): Have you ever watched a television show or movie and felt you could have written it better? Learn the secrets of successful screen writing. Gain the ability to influence people through characters and plot line. Find your original voice and tap into your own emotions. Learn how to write what is meaningful to you, and marketable to producers. Create an original series that could change the essence of today's television and movies.

Laugh Tracks (A53): Humour is associated with great intelligence. This introduction to comedic improvisation will help you gain confidence in your ability to perform spontaneously. You can make the most of your comedic talents while learning to loosen up, think quickly, and develop humorous characterizations. Great practice for developing intuition and teamwork skills too!

Broadway Beckons (A54): Sing! Dance! Act! The show will go on! Learn vocal techniques, dance and movement exercises, and character acting skills-all pertaining to a selected production. The class will present a mini-Broadway presentation at the end of the three weeks. Some recreation hour rehearsals may be required.

Two and Three-D Media: Drawing and Sculpting (A55): Express yourself in pencil, ink, watercolour, or three dimensions. Develop your techniques in perspective, light, shading, and colour theory. Learn the fundamentals of positive and negative space. Create an original work to be put on display.

Digital Photography (A56): Digital photography, a radically different technique from conventional photography, has changed the world of image recording. Learn how to enhance your own photographs to express yourself through a captured moment. If you like computers and cameras, this course is for you. You must bring your own digital camera to participate in this class. A 1G flash drive is highly recommended as well. Ages thirteen–seventeen only.

Fitness and Recreation Courses

All fitness and recreation courses are instructional and are for all ages ten through seventeen.

Getting in the Swim of Things (R57): Expert swimming instruction will be given at the beginning, intermediate, and advanced levels. A certified swimming instructor will help you improve your swimming skills. What a great way to chill out in the summer while you're getting in shape! Bring your goggles!

Gaming Through the Centuries: Winners Take All (R58): Learn a variety of games from Early American Games to new 21st Century games! Before television and the Wii, children played games that taught them how to aim, throw, and use their imaginations to solve problems! Take part in sack races and rolling the hoop! Fast-forward through time, learning games along the way like chuck-farthing and graces. End your journey with newer recreation, such as hacky sacks and Parkour! Create your own game with roots in games from history!

Fit for Life (R59): Enjoy your life to its fullest extent by being strong, healthy, and energetic. This course will help you do that through assessing your present state of fitness, making personal goals, individualizing your fitness activity according to your abilities, interests, needs and preferences, and learning more about the roles nutrition and emotion play in an overall approach to physical health. You'll exercise what you learn in the class and leave with a holistic approach to lifelong fitness.

Fencing: Foils to Epees (R60): Fencing-the mental prowess of chess, the grace of the athlete! Develop basic technique, form, finesse, and balance essential for success as a fencer. Refine your skills as you are paired with others of similar ability. The foil technique will emphasize a strong defence and body attack. Those who possess the skills will work with epees and sabers. Basic equipment will be provided.

Self-Defence Sense (R61): Self-defence strategies are important, not only in self-protection, but also in building physical and mental discipline. This class will help you present a commanding presence as you gain control and confidence through such strategies as awareness of your surroundings, wrist escapes, defence against body holds, and blocking. A healthy lifestyle is built on self-discipline, fitness and goal setting-the foundations of effective self-defence!

Appendix 3: Key events in the history of AIFS

1964   Founded by Cyril Taylor, Roger Walther and Doug Burck in Cincinnati, Ohio with Jimmy Corona in charge of the London office.
        First programme was for 1,500 US high school summer students in 1965.

1965   Moved to Greenwich, Connecticut.

1968   College programmes launched with programmes in Salamanca, Vichy, Grenoble, Schiller College near Stuttgart AIFS moves its offices to 102 Greenwich Avenue.

1969   AIFS was sold to National Student Marketing Corporation and acquired as a result, the Camp America programme.

1970   Hank Kahn joined the company and Doug Burck left to work for the Peace Corps in Peru. Cyril Taylor moved to London to oversee operations abroad.

1972   Richmond College in London purchased from the Methodist Missionary Society and a new university established.

1976   Roger Walther moved from Greenwich to San Francisco with Hank Kahn taking over in Greenwich.

1977   Cyril Taylor and Roger Walther repurchased AIFS from NSMC. Gordon Bennett joins AIFS in London.

1980   Bill Petrek appointed president of Richmond.

1981   Hank Kahn appointed to run the Greenwich office. John Linakis becomes VP Transportation in Greenwich.

1982   Partnership programmes first offered by the College Division.

1985   Bill Gertz joins the company as marketing director in Greenwich.
        Au Pair was launched with 475 participants. Lauren Kratovil joins the company to run Au Pair.

1987   Two major acquisitions were made this year. The American Council of International Study, a high school programme in Boston with 9,814 participants, whose chief executive was Mike Eizenberg, and the English Language Services (ELS) in Los Angeles, which ran English language programmes at a dozen US campuses with 18,716 participants, were purchased. Perry Akins was its chief operating officer.

1988   Bob Brennan succeeded Hank Kahn as president of AIFS and remained in the post until 31 December 2004.

1989   Enrolments in the high school division were devastated through drop-outs following the terrorist blowing up of the Pan Am jet over Lockerbie, Scotland.

1990   AIFS HS moved to Boston and combined with ACIS. AIFS America had its peak year with 8,613 enrolments.

1991   The First Gulf War badly affects enrolments.

1992   AIFS started its own insurance business, CISI, with coverage from the Virginia Surety Insurance Company. Home Stay in America programme was discontinued due to difficulty in finding families.
       The combined total of 66,021 participants in all programmes was the biggest in AIFS history. Mike DiMauro joins AIFS. Walter McCann became president of Richmond.

1993   A keystone year in the history of AIFS. Roger Walther agreed to exchange his shares in AIFS in return for the ownership of ELS.

1994   AIFS acquired the German agent GIJK, which later becomes AIFS Deutschland.

1995   AIFS launched its first website, www.aifs.com.

1996   Au Pair enrolments increased due to the US State Department opening up recruitment from just Western Europe to the whole world. Marcie Schneider joined the company in London to run Au Pair in America. Thomas Kiechle joined the company to run AIFS Deutschland.

1997   Peter Jones became president of ACIS upon the retirement of Mike Eizenberg.

1998   Mike Berry joined the company as vice president, finance.

2000   AIFS bought the Summer Institute for the Gifted from Philip Zipse.
       The first online matching system for Au Pairs is introduced.

2001   The total number of AIFS alumni reached 1 million participants.
       CareMed Insurance purchased in Germany.
       A devastating impact on High School enrolment was caused by the 9/11 attacks on the World Trade Center in New York.
       Norman Smith became president of Richmond. Stephen Gessner became president of SIG. Barbara Swicord appointed as SIG's academic director, becoming president in 2007.

2003   CISI-BOLDUC business purchased.
       Prospective counsellors are able to apply online for the Camp America Programme.

2004   Bob Brennan retired as president in December and his place is taken by Bill Gertz.

2009   Enrolment was badly affected by the world economic crisis.
       Worse affected were Au Pair, High School, Camp America and College programmes. However, despite the decline in enrolment, AIFS still enrolled 36,000 students and had a successful year financially.

2010   Enrolments have recovered and AIFS celebrated the enrolment of 1.5 million students since 1965.

Appendix 4: Purchase agreement with the Methodist Church for the purchase of Richmond College by AIFS

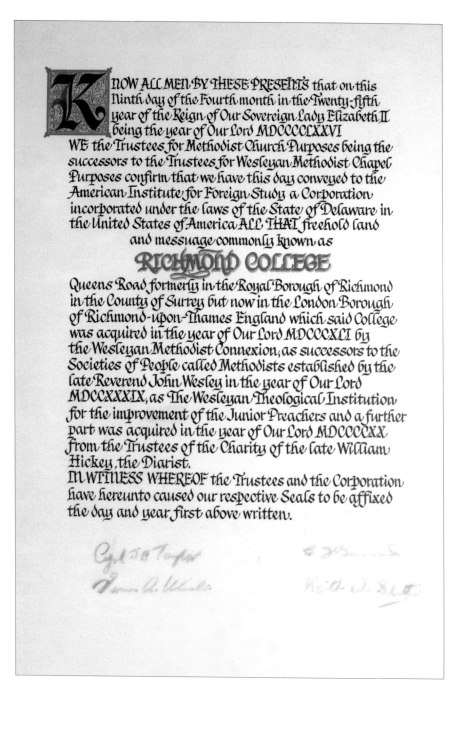

KNOW ALL MEN BY THESE PRESENTS that on this Ninth day of the Fourth month in the Twenty-fifth year of the Reign of Our Sovereign Lady Elizabeth II being the year of Our Lord MDCCCCLXXVI WE the Trustees for Methodist Church Purposes being the successors to the Trustees for Wesleyan Methodist Chapel Purposes confirm that we have this day conveyed to the American Institute for Foreign Study a Corporation incorporated under the laws of the State of Delaware in the United States of America ALL THAT freehold land and messuage commonly known as

RICHMOND COLLEGE

Queens Road formerly in the Royal Borough of Richmond in the County of Surrey but now in the London Borough of Richmond-upon-Thames England which said College was acquired in the year of Our Lord MDCCCXLI by the Wesleyan Methodist Connexion, as successors to the Societies of People called Methodists established by the late Reverend John Wesley in the year of Our Lord MDCCXXXIX, as The Wesleyan Theological Institution for the improvement of the Junior Preachers and a further part was acquired in the year of Our Lord MDCCCCXX from the Trustees of the Charity of the late William Hickey, the Diarist.

IN WITNESS WHEREOF the Trustees and the Corporation have hereunto caused our respective Seals to be affixed the day and year first above written.

Appendix 5: Letter from Prime Minister Thatcher in 1990 supporting the launch of the Specialist Schools initiative

10 DOWNING STREET

LONDON SW1A 2AA

THE PRIME MINISTER   22 February 1990

Dear Sir Cyril,

I was pleased to receive the very interesting report in your letter of 15 January of developments within the City Technology College Programme. Thank you for sending me the well produced publicity material and video of the Macmillan CTC.

I was interested to hear of the proposal for an extension of the CTC Programme at lower unit cost by way of voluntary-aided CTCs. I am most grateful to you and to other members of the Trust for the work you have done to identify means of extending CTC benefits more widely into the maintained sector. I am sure that you will make a convincing case to potential sponsors whose support will be vital. Meanwhile, both the Secretary of State and I, as you know, would like to see some higher pro rata contributions from sponsors to existing CTC projects. I was encouraged to hear that two major sponsors have already agreed to join forces on one project. I hope that you will encourage others to do likewise and support other efforts to increase the private sector investment in these colleges. I hope too that, if a decision is made to proceed with VA CTCs, committed LEAs will also be prepared to make a significant contribution to the capital costs of the conversion of existing schools to CTCs, as an investment in the upgrading of secondary education in their areas.

- 2 -

An equal partnership between Government, LEAs and business sponsors would be an excellent signal to the maintained sector more generally in encouraging the replication of CTC standards and achievements across secondary provision. I am grateful to you for the part you have played in identifying the possibility of wider development.

Yours sincerely

Margaret Thatcher

Sir Cyril Taylor

Appendix 6: Letter from Prime Minister John Major in September 1993 congratulating Cyril Taylor on the successful launch of the specialist schools

10 DOWNING STREET
LONDON SW1A 2AA

THE PRIME MINISTER

27 September 1993

John Patten has told me of the launch of the new Technology College initiative. I know how much its existence, and the number of prospective sponsors, owe to your efforts and interest. I am delighted to see how well CTCs are now being accepted as a permanent part of the education scene, and wish you every success with this latest scheme.

With many thanks for all you do,

Sir Cyril Taylor

Appendix 7: List of Secretaries of State for Education for whom I served as special adviser

Below is a list of the ten Education Secretaries appointed from May 1980 until June 2007 with whom I worked as a special adviser:

Kenneth Baker   May 1986–July 1989 (3 years 2 months).
John MacGregor   August 1989–October 1990 (15 months).
Kenneth Clarke   November 1990–April 1992 (17 months).
John Patten   May 1992–September 1994 (2 years 4 months).
Gillian Shepherd   September 1994–May 1997 (2 years 8 months).
David Blunkett   May 1997–June 2001 (4 years 1 month).
Estelle Morris   May 2001–October 2002 (17 months).

Charles Clarke	October 2002–December 2004 (2 years, 2 months).
Ruth Kelly	December 2004–May 2006 (17 months).
Alan Johnson	May 2006–June 2007 (13 months).

Prime Ministers during the same period:

Margaret Thatcher	1979–1990.
John Major	1990–1997.
Tony Blair	1997–2007.

Appendix 8: List of GBE members

Serial	Name	Date of appointment
	Grand Master: HRH Prince Philip, The Duke of Edinburgh	
1	The Right Hon Sir Ronald Davison GBE CMG	11/02/1978
2	Air Chief Marshal Sir Peter Le Cheminant GBE KCB DFC*	03/06/1978
3	The Hon Sir Yuet-keung Kan GBE JP	16/06/1979
4	General Sir Hugh Beach GBE KCB MC	31/12/1979
5	Sir Christopher Leaver GBE JP	21/10/1981
6	Sir Anthony Jolliffe GBE DL	06/10/1982
7	Sir Alan Traill GBE QSO	09/10/1984
8	General Sir Frank Kitson GBE KCB MC* DL	31/12/1984
9	Sir David Rowe-Ham GBE	07/10/1986
10	Sir Kenneth Newman GBE QPM	13/06/1987
11	Sir Greville Spratt GBE TD DL JP	07/10/1987
12	Sir Christopher Collett GBE JP	06/10/1988
13	Sir Sze-yuen Chung GBE DSc PhD JP	31/12/1988
14	Air Chief Marshal Sir David Harcourt-Smith GBE KCB DFC	31/12/1988

15	The Right Hon Sir Thomas Eichelbaum GBE	06/02/1989
16	Admiral Sir John Woodward GBE KCB	17/06/1989
17	Sir Hugh Bidwell GBE	10/10/1989
18	Field Marshal The Lord Vincent of Coleshill GBE KCB DSO	30/12/1989
19	Sir Alexander Graham GBE DCL	09/10/1990
20	Admiral Sir Jeremy Black GBE KCB DSO	15/06/1991
21	Air Chief Marshal Sir Patrick Hine GCB GBE	29/06/1991
22	Sir Brian Jenkins GBE	08/10/1991
23	Air Chief Marshal Sir Anthony Skingsley GBE KCB	31/12/1991
24	Sir Francis McWilliams GBE	05/10/1992
25	Admiral Sir Kenneth Eaton GBE KCB	31/12/1993
26	The Right Hon Lord Rothschild OM GBE	31/12/1997
27	Air Chief Marshal Sir William Wratten GBE CB AFC	31/12/1997
28	Admiral Sir Peter Abbott GBE KCB	31/12/1998
29	The Right Hon Sir Stephen Brown GBE	12/06/1999
30	Sir Michael Perry GBE	31/12/2001
31	Air Chief Marshal Sir Anthony Bagnall GBE KCB FRAeS	31/12/2002
32	Sir Cyril Taylor GBE	31/12/2003
33	Sir Bryan Nicholson GBE	31/12/2004
34	The Right Honourable Baroness Butler-Sloss GBE	31/12/2004
35	General Sir Timothy Granville-Chapman GBE KCB	30/12/2006

36	Sir David Cooksey GBE	16/06/2007
37	The Earl of Selborne GBE FRS	January 2011
38	Lord Weidenfeld GBE	January 2011
39	Professor Sir Mervyn King GBE	June 2011
40	The Right Honourable Lady Hayman GBE	January 2012
41	Sir (Thomas) John Parker	16/06/12

Appendix 9: Copy of letter from Tony Blair congratulating Cyril Taylor on his work as chair of the Specialist Schools and Academies Trust

10 DOWNING STREET
LONDON SW1A 2AA

THE PRIME MINISTER

9 February 2004

Dear Cyril,

Thank you for your letter and your kind remarks, which were much appreciated.

Your honour in the New Year list was a fitting recognition of the magnificent work you have done over the years in building up the specialist school movement. Nothing is more important to the development of a world class education system, and I am glad that you remain as committed as ever.

With warm personal regards,

yours ever,

Tony

Sir Cyril Taylor GBE

Appendix 10: Copy of letter from Prime Minister Gordon Brown thanking Cyril Taylor for his work in improving standards in English schools

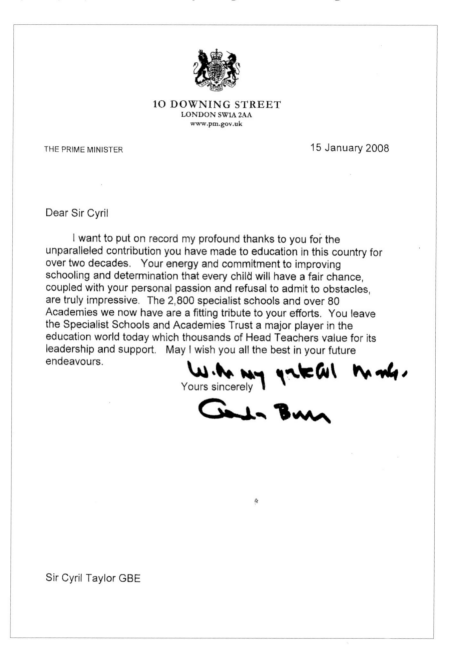

10 DOWNING STREET
LONDON SW1A 2AA
www.pm.gov.uk

THE PRIME MINISTER   15 January 2008

Dear Sir Cyril

    I want to put on record my profound thanks to you for the unparalleled contribution you have made to education in this country for over two decades. Your energy and commitment to improving schooling and determination that every child will have a fair chance, coupled with your personal passion and refusal to admit to obstacles, are truly impressive. The 2,800 specialist schools and over 80 Academies we now have are a fitting tribute to your efforts. You leave the Specialist Schools and Academies Trust a major player in the education world today which thousands of Head Teachers value for its leadership and support. May I wish you all the best in your future endeavours.

Yours sincerely

Sir Cyril Taylor GBE

Appendix 11: Brief for sponsors of specialist schools

December 2007
Specialist Schools: A general brief for sponsors and schools
Ninety-three percent of all secondary schools in England now have specialist or academy status. The 2,799 specialist schools and eighty-three Academies are maintained English secondary schools which teach the full national curriculum but give particular attention to their specialist subject, sometimes through an extended school day. All maintained secondary schools are eligible to bid for specialist status. There is no government cap on the number of specialist schools and funding is available for every approved bid.

Each prospective specialist school must obtain sponsorship of £50,000 or more from the private sector. A special Department for Education and Skills partnership fund has been established with the help of the Garfield Weston Foundation to assist schools who find it difficult to raise the full £50,000 sponsorship. Though sponsorship is a one-off charitable contribution, sponsors are encouraged to become involved with their school, either through joining the governing body or offering pupils and teachers work experience or other encouragement. Over the last two years, Sept 05/Sept 07, 627 schools have been designated, but there are still some 400 schools who have yet to achieve specialist status.

Schools applying for specialist school status submit a detailed development plan to the DfES with specific targets for improving the school's overall results and raising achievement in the specialist subject. This plan also shows how one third of the extra funding to be received will be used to help other schools, especially feeder primary schools, in their local community.

Successful applicants initially receive a one-off government capital grant of £100,000 together with an annual top up recurrent grant of £129 per pupil for three years, equivalent to about £129,000 for the average sized school of 1,000 pupils. This is equivalent to about 3 per cent of their normal recurrent funding. Thus an investment of £50,000 in sponsorship attracts an initial government grant for each school of approximately £500,000, a leverage of ten to one. Donations are tax deductible in both the UK and the USA.

Specialist schools must apply for re-designation every three years. Re-designation is now linked to the regular Ofsted inspection cycle of schools. Schools which receive a grade 1 or 2 from Ofsted are automatically re-designated. Schools receiving a grade of 3 are usually re-designated subject to a review of their performance by the Department for Education. Schools given a grade 4, which puts a school into special measures or under notice to improve, are placed on probation and may ultimately lose their designation but can reapply for designation once improvements have been achieved.

Schools applying for redesignation as a specialist school may, if they wish, apply for a further capital grant of £25,000 from the Department, providing they raise sponsorship of a similar amount and agree to enter into a partnership with one or more local employers.

Schools meeting published High Performing Specialist Schools criteria are given high performing specialist status. These schools are eligible to either add a second curriculum specialism, the vocational option or Special Educational Needs specialism, apply for training school status or to help an under-performing school. Additional grants for high performing schools of between £60 to £90 per pupil per year are paid to these schools.

The mission of specialist schools

The mission of specialist schools is to build a world-class network of innovative, high performing secondary schools. These schools, working in partnership with business and the wider community, bring choice and diversity to the English maintained secondary school system. This initiative is first and foremost focussed on raising standards of overall achievement. Specialist schools have high expectations of their pupils and create an ethos of discipline, order and achievement. They seek to ensure that young people are well-educated and technologically skilled, ready and able to progress into employment, further training or higher education according to their individual abilities, aptitudes and ambitions. They add to the richness and variety of secondary school provision, acting as a resource for neighbouring schools and the local community.

The 2,882 specialist schools and academies educate 3 million pupils, 90 per cent of all English secondary school pupils in maintained schools, to an increasingly high standard.

There are eleven different types of specialist school:

Technology Colleges (currently 569) specialise in teaching mathematics, science, design technology, and information & communications technology (ICT);

Arts Colleges (currently 457) specialise in teaching all the performing arts (including music, dance and drama, visual or media arts);

Sports Colleges (currently 370) specialise in teaching physical education and sport, and also serve as centres of sporting excellence for neighbouring schools;

Science Colleges (currently 310) emphasise the study of physics, chemistry and biology, working with leading university science departments, industry and major UK science bodies to create innovative centres of excellence;

Mathematics & Computing Colleges (currently 259) emphasise these two essential prerequisites for further studies in the sciences and technology and for jobs requiring numerical analysis;

Business & Enterprise Colleges (currently 243) specialise in business studies and foster an enterprise culture in schools. They teach business studies, financial literacy, enterprise-related vocational studies and marketing skills;

Language Colleges (currently 218) specialise in teaching modern foreign languages and promote an international ethos across the whole curriculum;

Humanities Colleges (currently 108) specialise in either English (both language and literature) history or geography and foster an understanding of human values and attitudes;

Engineering Colleges (currently 55) focus on mathematics and design technology, providing opportunities to study a wide range of engineering disciplines from civil and electrical engineering to telecoms. Their aim is to increase the number of good applicants for engineering degrees;

Music Colleges (currently 24) specialise in teaching music but also have a secondary focus on mathematics or ICT;

SEN specialism (currently 70). A total of 120 special schools have so far achieved specialist status, with the balance opting for subject specialism.

There are 116 schools with combined specialisms. Additionally schools in

rural areas may add a rural dimension in any of the above specialisms.
There are eighty-three academies currently open, and two City Technology
Colleges which have decided not to apply for academy status. Academies
specialise in a variety of subjects.

Role of Sponsors
Sponsors of Specialist Schools, either individually, or collectively with other
sponsors, provide the following assistance:

A one-time financial contribution which totals at least £50,000 per school.
Donations are deductible against tax in both the UK and the USA and can be
given either in cash or in suitable kind but cannot be conditional upon purchase
of the sponsors' products. There is no ongoing obligation to provide additional
financial assistance;
Sponsors are encouraged (but not required) to enter into long-term support
relationships with their school. This may include one or more of the
following:

Appointing governors to serve on the school's governing body;
Encouraging the schools to report annually on their progress;
Providing work placements for teachers and students, providing careers
advice for students and mentoring of both students and teachers.

Above all, sponsors are invited to help schools develop a businesslike ethos
which encourages delivery of a high-quality education and value for money.
Some sponsors enter into long-term funding agreements (three years or more)
under which a number of schools are supported over a period of time. Over
the past twenty years, 600 sponsors have contributed over £300 million of
sponsorship to specialist schools and academies.
Record of Specialist Schools
The record of specialist schools in raising standards is impressive.
    In 2007, the half millions students in specialist schools achieved 62.3% 5
+ A*–C grades at GCSE. The compares to 60.6% in 2006 and is an increase
of more than a third over the past ten years.
Specialist schools averaged 48.3% 5 + A*–C grates including Maths and
English in 2007. This compares to 47.2% in 2006.
Research by Professor David Jesson of York University, shows that specialist
schools regularly achieve a higher actual performance than their intakes of
ability at age 11 would predict.
The success of the specialist schools programme has led the Confederation
of British Industry, the Institute of Directors and the Engineering Employers'
Federation as well as many leading firms and distinguished foundations to
endorse the programme.

> The CBI formally endorses the specialist schools programme as a key
> contributor to raising educational standards and improving the skills
> base of the UK. It encourages its members to become involved in
> partnerships with education in whatever way is most appropriate for
> the business concerned.
> The Confederation of British Industry

The IoD endorses the specialist schools programme as an outstanding example of effective business/school links. We would encourage our members to support specialist schools through sponsorship, appointment of business governors or through the provision of work experience for both teachers and pupils.
Institute of Directors

A recent evaluation by Ofsted says that specialist schools are performing better and improving faster than other schools. David Bell, writing in 2005 as Her Majesty's Chief Inspector of Schools, said, 'Being a specialist school makes a difference. Working to declared targets, dynamic leadership, a renewed sense of purpose, targeted use of funding and being a contributor to an optimistic network of like-minded schools, all contribute to a climate for improvement and drive forward change.'

Application Process
Applications for specialist school status are made to the Specialist Schools Unit at the DfES. For detailed guidance, see DfES generic guidance setting out the criteria for all specialist schools (and combinations) plus separate sections for each of the ten specialisms at www.standards.dfes.gov.uk/ specialistschools. The application should contain the following:

Information about the school, including size, legal status and recent examination results;
A development plan to achieve measurable improvements both in the specialist subjects and overall, to include quantified performance targets to be achieved over the four year period;
Evidence of how the school will work with other schools and the wider community;
An outline of the bid for capital grant from the DfES, (grants may be used for the purchase of equipment, furniture and associated building work in order to enhance facilities for the teaching of the specialist subjects).
An outline of how the recurrent grant would support the development plan;
Details of sponsorship confirmed. The details of the proposed on-going partnerships with sponsors, including co-option on to the governing body.

There are normally two application rounds for specialist schools each year, in March and October.
Role of the Specialist Schools and Academies Trust and the Youth Sport Trust
The Specialist Schools and Academies Trust is the lead advisory body on the specialist school initiative for the DfES, providing advice and support for schools seeking to achieve or maintain specialist school status. See their website: wwwssatrust.org.uk. Founded in 1987, the Specialist Schools and Academies Trust is a registered educational charity which has 300 staff and is funded by fees from its 3,000 affiliated schools, donations from sponsors and foundations, and grants from the DfES. Its work includes the promotion and support of specialist schools' and academies' curriculum development and innovation, teacher training in ICT, conference and seminar activities and a publications programme. The Specialist Schools and Academies Trust

plays an important role in raising sponsorship and introducing potential sponsors to suitable candidate schools. The Youth Sport Trust supports schools seeking Sports College status (www.youthsporttrust.org).

Further Information

For more information about any of the sponsorship opportunities outlined, please contact:

Sue Williamson, Director and Chief Executive SSAT (The Schools Network), 5th Floor, Central House, 142 Central Street, London ECIV 8AR.

Tel: +44 (0) 20 7802 2300 Fax: +44 (0) 20 7802 2345

Email: sue.williamson@ssatuk.co.uk Website: ssatuk.co.uk

COMPANY NO. 8073410.

Appendix 12: Front cover of original AIFS brochure in 1964

Appendix 13: Chart showing the basic structure of German secondary education

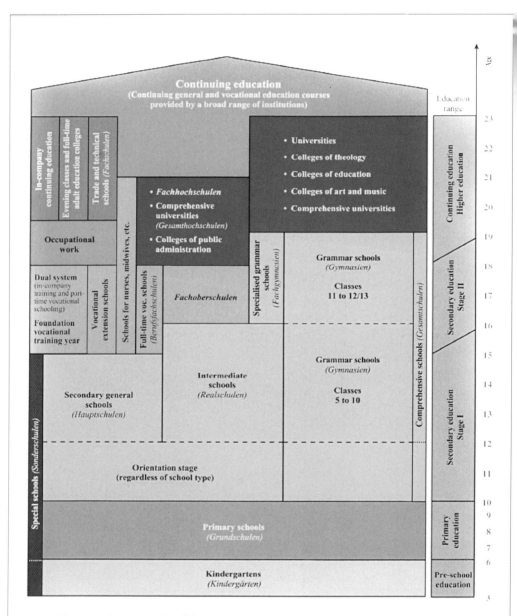

- Diagrammatic representation of the typical structure of the education system in the Federal Republic of Germany. In individual *Länder* there are variations from the above pattern.
- The age given for attendance at the various educational institutions refers to the earliest possible typical entry.

Source: Based on BMBF, 2004

Appendix 14: Fund-raising brochure of the British Friends of Harvard Business School

Background

The British Friends of HBS was set up in 1992 by the HBS Club of London as a British registered charity to raise scholarship funds for financially needy British students to attend Harvard Business School.

Since 1992 the British Friends have awarded forty-four tuition scholarships totalling over £633,902.

The Scholarship Fund provides an invaluable source of financial aid to students who otherwise could not pay for the cost of attending Harvard Business School. All scholarship recipients are selected through the rigorous Fulbright selection process and are then chosen on a financial needs basis and give a commitment to return to the UK at the end of their MBA. Successful recipients also give an undertaking to contribute to the Scholarship Fund when their circumstances permit. The scholarships are awarded jointly with the Fulbright Commission and go towards funding first-year tuition costs.

All donations to the British Friends are deductible against UK tax under the Gift Aid Scheme providing that person pays UK taxes.

All donations to the British Friends Scholarship Fund will count towards section and class reunion fund-raising and annual lists of donations at HBS.

To make a donation send your cheque made out to 'British Friends of Harvard Business School' and fill out the gift aid form (which will be sent to you). The British Friends will obtain the tax refund and add this amount to the donation and inform Harvard Business School who will credit the appropriate class/reunion section. Please note the British Friends charges no administration fee for doing this.

Please specify if you wish your donation to remain with the Scholarship Fund or transferred to the school for an appropriate educational purpose).

If you are a dual UK/US tax payer see below section on giving through the CAF American Donor Fund.

Gifts Direct to School

The English Charity Commissioners have agreed that UK residents paying UK tax can make gifts for the benefit of Harvard Business School through the British Friends for appropriate educational purposes and claim UK tax relief on their donations.

Tax-Effective Giving for Dual-Registered (UK and US) Taxpayers

British Friends of HBS

The British Friends is now approved by the CAF Donor's Fund Eligibility Committee to receive grants. For dual US-UK tax payers giving through the CAF American Donor Fund allows donors to get a tax deduction in both the US and UK. Donor can give through the CAF American Donor Fund if they pay tax in both the UK and US and if earnings exceed the worldwide foreign-earned income threshold (currently $80,000).

For more information and Gift forms see the below website link, or request information from the British Friends of HBS http://www.cafonline.org/default. aspx?page=7141&btnServices=&.

If you choose to donate using this vehicle, please let us know and your class/

reunion year so that we can let the school know and ensure you are given the appropriate credit. Please note that CAF charge an admin fee so the amount donated to the British Friends will not be the same as sent to CAF.

Patrons
Sir Ronald Cohen, MBA 69
David Dutton, MBA 69
Bruno Schroder, MBA 60
Sir Martin Sorrell, MBA 68

Trustees
Sir Cyril Taylor, GBE, MBA 61
Chairman
Bruno Schroder, MBA 60
Vice Chairman
Neil Meadows, MBA 94
Treasurer
Susan Hamilton
Director, International Relations
Harvard Business School
Penny Egan
Ex officio, Executive Director
The UK US Fulbright Commission
Jean Gomm, MBA 72
Ex officio, President, HBS Club of London
Robert J Brown, MBA 66
Vincent Dessain, MBA 87
Charles Lazarevic, AMP 161
Jeremy Mayhew, MBA 89
George Newell, MBA 63
Anthony Rosenfelder, MBA 73
Stuart Rolland, MBA 91

Donations should be sent to the following address for processing:

British Friends of Harvard Business School
37 Queen's Gate, London SW7 5HR
www.bfhbs.org

Appendix 15: Presidents of Richmond, the American International University in London

1972–1975	Anthony Lonsdale (Principal)
1975–1980	Vernon Mealor (Principal)
1980–1992	Dr William Petrek (President)
1992–2002	Dr Walter McCann (President)
2002–2007	Dr Norman Smith (President)
2007–2008	Dr Jos Hackforth-Jones (Interim President)
2008–2011	Dr Ian Newbould (President)
2011–	Dr John Annette (President)

Appendix 16: Honorary degree recipients of Richmond, the American International University in London

1992
Dr Raymond G. H. Seitz
Former Ambassador of the United States of America to the Court of St James
Doctor of Public Administration
Dr William Petrek (deceased)
Former President, Richmond, The American International University in London
Doctor of Humane Letters

1993
The Lord Renwick of Clifton KCMG
Former Her Majesty's Ambassador to Washington
Doctor of Laws
The Lord Briggs of Lewes
Chairman Emeritus of the Board of Academic Governors, Richmond The American International University in London
Former Chancellor, The Open University
Former Provost, Worcester College, Oxford
Former Vice-Chancellor, Sussex University
Doctor of Literature
Professor Sir Ernst Gombrich (deceased)
Director Emeritus of the Warburg Institute, University of London
Former Academic Governor
Richmond, The American International University in London
Doctor of Literature
The Lord Marshall of Knightsbridge (deceased)
Former Chairman, British Airways Plc
Doctor of Laws

1994
The Rt Hon. The Lord Baker of Dorking CH
Former Secretary of State for Education and Science
Doctor of Laws
Dr Michael Morgan
Former Principal, The Froebel Educational Institute, London
Trustee Emeritus, Richmond, The American International University in London
Doctor of Literature
Professor The Lord Quirk of Bloomsbury CBE, FBA
Trustee, The Wolfson Foundation
Former President, British Academy
Former Vice-Chancellor, University of London
Former Academic Governor
Richmond, The American International University in London
Doctor of Literature
The Lord Attenborough of Richmond upon Thames CBE
Performing Arts Director and Actor
Doctor of Literature
Dr Lawrence Tindale (deceased)

Former Deputy Chairman, 3i plc
Former Trustee, Richmond, The American International University in London
Doctor of Laws
Dr Donald Woods (deceased)
International Lecturer and Broadcaster
Doctor of Literature

1995
Dr Robert J. Brennan (deceased)
Chairman, Metro International
Trustee, Richmond, The American International University in London
Doctor of Business Administration
The Lord Sutherland of Houndwood KT
Former Vice-Chancellor, University of London
Former Principal and Vice-Chancellor, University of Edinburgh
Doctor of Literature
Dr Garry Weston (deceased)
Former Chairman, Associated British Foods Plc
Doctor of Economics
Dr William J. Crowe Jr
Former Ambassador of the United States of America to the Court of St James
Doctor of International Relations
Dr Michael Eizenberg
Former President, American Council for International Studies
Former Trustee, Richmond, The American International University in London
Doctor of Business Administration
Dr Stephen J. Trachtenberg
Former President & Professor of Public Administration
The George Washington University
Doctor of Laws

1996
The Lord Harris of Peckham KT
Chairman, Carpetright plc
Doctor of Economics
Dr Kathleen Kennedy Townsend
Former Lieutenant Governor, State of Maryland
Doctor of Laws
Dr Edwin M. Yoder Jr
Columnist, The Washington Post Writers Group
Professor of Journalism & Humanities, Washington & Lee University,
Lexington
Doctor of Letters
Sir Stanley Kalms KT
President, Dixons Group plc
Doctor of Economics
Dr Herbert Kretzmer
Journalist and Lyricist
Doctor of Letters
Dr Hans Rausing

Former Chairman & CEO, Tetra Laval Group
Doctor of Economics

1997
Dr Anastasios Christodoulou CBE (deceased)
Former Secretary-General, Association of Commonwealth Universities
Former Trustee, Richmond, The American International University in London
Doctor of International Relations
Dr Stephen R. Portch
Former Chancellor, Board of Regents of the University System of Georgia
Doctor of Literature
Dr Rasha Al-Sabah
Under Secretary, Ministry of Higher Education, Kuwait
Doctor of Laws
Dr Eve Arnold OBE (deceased)
Photographer
Doctor of Humanities
Sir John Daniel KT
Assistant Director-General for Education, UNESCO
Former Vice-Chancellor, The Open University
Doctor of Humane Letters
Professor Stanley Glasser
Emeritus Professor of Music, University of London
Academic Governor, Richmond, The American International University in London
Doctor of Music
Sir Cyril Taylor GBE
Chairman, American Institute for Foreign Study
Founder & Chairman of the Specialist Schools & Academic Trust (1987–2005)
Doctor of Laws

1998
Sir John Bond KT
Group Chairman, HSBC Holdings plc
Doctor of Economics
Senator Zell Miller
Former Governor of the State of Georgia
Former United States Senator for the State of Georgia
Doctor of Laws
Sir Joseph Rotblat KCMG (deceased)
Physicist
Doctor of International Relations
Dr John Brademas
President Emeritus of New York University
Doctor of Laws
Professor Malcolm Frazer CBE
Former Chief Executive, Council for National Academic Awards
Doctor of Education
Dr Alfredo Gomez Gil
Professor and Poet
Doctor of Literature

1999

The Hon. Philip Lader
Former Ambassador of the United States of America to the Court of St James
Doctor of Laws
Sir Colin Southgate KT
Former Chairman, EMI Group Plc
Former Chairman, The Royal Opera House, Covent Garden
Doctor of Economics
Dr Zoe Wanamaker
Actor
Doctor of Letters
Dr Clifford D. Joseph
Barrister-at-Law
Trustee, Richmond, The American International University in London
Doctor of Laws
Sir Mark Tully KBE
Freelance Journalist and Broadcaster
Doctor of Communications

2000

Dr Helen Bamber OBE
Founder & Director, Medical Foundation for the Care of Victims of Torture
Doctor of Humanities
The Lord Puttnam CBE
Film Producer
Doctor of Fine Arts
Dr Roger Walther
Chairman, First Republic Bank
Chairman & CEO, Tusker Corporation
Doctor of Economics
Dr George Steven Blumenthal
Former Chairman, NTL Inc.
Doctor of Communications and Information Technology
Dr Nemir A. Kirdar
Founder, President & CEO of Investcorp
Doctor of Economics
Dr Anthony Taylor
Former Trustee
Richmond, The American International University in London
Doctor of Economics

2001

Ambassador Harriet Elam-Thomas (retired)
Former Ambassador of the United States of America to the Republic of Senegal
Doctor of Laws
Professor The Baroness Greenfield CBE
Professor of Pharmacology, Oxford University
Director, Royal Institution of Great Britain
Doctor of Science

Dr James Ragan
Poet
Doctor of Letters
The Earl of Limerick (deceased)
Former Chancellor, London Guildhall University
Doctor of Laws
Dr John Morgridge
Chairman Emeritus, Cisco Systems Inc.
Doctor of Economics
The Rt Hon. The Lord Woolf
Former Lord Chief Justice of England and Wales
Doctor of Laws

2002
Dr Walter McCann
Former President
Richmond, The American International University in London
Doctor of Laws
Dr Alba Ambert
Former Writer in Residence
Richmond, The American International University in London
Doctor of Literature
Dr Richard Resch
Former Provost & Senior Vice President for Academic Affairs
Richmond, The American International University in London
Doctor of Science
Dr John Fairbairn
Trustee, Esmee Fairbairn Foundation
Doctor of Humane Letters
Dame Pauline Harris DBE
Trustee, Philip & Pauline Harris Charitable Trust
Doctor of Humane Letters
Dr John Kuhnle
Managing Director Education Practice, Korn/Ferry International
Trustee Emeritus
Richmond, The American International University in London
Doctor of Humane Letters

2003
Dr Deborah McLean
Vice Chairman of the Board of Trustees
Richmond, The American International University in London
Doctor of Humane Letters
Professor Graham Zellick
Former Vice-Chancellor, University of London
Doctor of Laws
The Rt Hon. Michael Portillo
Former Member of Parliament for Kensington & Chelsea
Doctor of Laws

2004
Dr Vivian Day Stroh
Alumna & Trustee
Richmond, The American International University in London
Doctor of Humane Letters
Dr Laura H. Harris
Alumna and Former Trustee
Richmond, The American International University in London
Doctor of Humane Letters
Professor Brenda M. Gourley
Vice-Chancellor, The Open University
Doctor of Humane Letters

2005
Dr Russel R. Taylor
Trustee Emeritus
Richmond, The American International University in London
Doctor of Humane Letters
Dr Robert W. Selander
President and CEO of Mastercard International
Doctor International Business
Professor Sir Christopher Frayling
Rector and Vice-Provost, Royal College of Art
Chairman, Arts Council England
Doctor of Humane Letters

2006
The Baroness Deech DBE
Independent Adjudicator for Higher Education
Doctor of Laws
Dr Amelia Chilcott Fawcett CBE
Former Vice-Chairman, Morgan Stanley International
Doctor of International Business
Dr David Hempleman-Adams MBE, OBE
Explorer, Cold Climate Expeditions Ltd
Doctor of Science

2007
The Lord Watson of Richmond CBE
Chairman, The Cambridge Foundation
Chairman, CTN Communications
Trustee, Richmond The American International University in London
Doctor of Humane Letters
Dr Anthony Seldon
Master of Wellington College
Doctor of Humane Letters
Dame Mary Richardson
Chief Executive, HSBC Trust (retired)
Doctor of Humane Letters
Dr William Mules (retired)

Former Head of the American School in London
Doctor of Humane Letters

2008
Dr Lionel Barber
Editor, *The Financial Times*
Doctor of Humane Letters
Dr Norman R. Smith
Former President, Richmond The American International University in London
Doctor of Education
Sir Sigmund Sternberg
Co-founder, The Three Faiths Forum
Doctor of Humane Letters
Professor Alice Tomic
Intercultural Communications Specialist
Doctor of Humane Letters

2009
Professor Jos Hackforth-Jones
Director, Sotheby's Institute of Art, London
Doctor of Fine Arts
Sir Robert Worcester KBE DL
Chairman, Ipsos Group, Chairman & Founder of MORI
Doctor of Laws

2010
George Garfield Weston
Chief Executive, Associated British Foods plc
Doctor of Laws
Mariam Assefa
Executive Director & CEO
World Education Services, New York
Doctor of Laws

2011
Kevin Everett
Chairman of the Board, Sir John Cass's Foundation
Doctor of Business Administration
Professor Julia Jeannet (deceased)
Founder of the Foundations Program
Richmond, The American International University in London
Doctor of Humane Letters
Deirdre Simpson
Former Director Alumni Relations
Richmond, The American International University in London
Doctor of Laws

2012
Lord Adonis
Chair, Progress

Doctor of Public Administration
Professor Robert Leppard
Former Provost & Special Advisor to the President
Richmond, The American International University in London
Doctor of Business Administration

Appendix 17: Publications by Cyril Taylor

One of my favourite activities was to write political papers and indeed books. In 1972, together with Julian Radcliffe, I wrote my first political policy paper, 'Peace Has Its Price', published by the Bow Group. Since 1969, I have written the following books and papers:

The Guide to Study Abroad, Co-author with Professor John A. Garraty of Columbia University and a famous historian, and Lily von Klemperer, director of the Institute of International Education, published by Harper & Row (several editions with the first edition in 1969).
Peace Has Its Price, published by the Bow Group in 1972.
No More Tick, Co-author with Alan Walters and Peter Lilley, published by the Bow Group, 1974.
The Elected Member's Guide to Reducing Public Expenditure, published by Conservative Political Centre, 1980.
A Realistic Plan for London Transport, published by the Bow Group in 1982.
Reforming London's Government, published by the Bow Group, March 1984.
London Preserv'd, published by the Bow Group, January 1985.
Bringing Accountability Back to Local Government, published by the Centre for Policy Studies, April 1985.
Employment Examined: the Right Approach to More Jobs, published by the Centre for Policy Studies, May 1986. This paper recommended setting up the original City Technology Colleges.
Raising Educational Standards: a Personal Perspective, published by the Centre for Policy Studies, November 1990.
The Future of Higher Education, Co-Author, published by the Conservative Political Centre, 1996.
Value Added in Specialist Schools 1999, 2000, 2001, 2002, 2003, 2004, 2005, 2006, Co Author with Professor David Jesson, published by the Specialist Schools Trust.
Excellence in Education: the Making of Great Schools, Co-Author with Conor Ryan (published by Fulton Press) in November 2004, with a revised edition in 2005.
Who Will Champion Our Vulnerable Children, published in 2006 by the Specialist Schools and Academies Trust. A study of the necessity of improving the support given to children in care.
Education, Education, Education, Ten Years On, Co-author with Prime Minister Tony Blair and Liz Reid, published by the Specialist Schools & Academies Trust in 2007.
A Good School for Every Child, published by Routledge in 2009. See picture taken at the book launch in 2009.
How English Universities Could Learn from the American Higher Education System, published by the Institute of Economic Affairs in 2009.

Appendix 18: The American Institute for Foreign Study: ethos and divisions

AIFS has a clear mission, which is:

> To provide the highest quality educational and cultural exchanges to enrich the lives
> of young people throughout the world and to bring the world together.

95 per cent of our students rate their experience with us as excellent or good.
We are committed to the following values:

First-rate leadership;
Excellence in operations, people;
Respect and understanding of different cultures;
Exceptional caring support for our participants to ensure their safety and well-being;
Honest, equitable and non-discriminatory treatment of participants, partners and employees;
Technological innovation;
Teamwork and collaboration both within the organisation and with partners;
Encouragement of employee initiative and professional development;
Responsible financial stewardship.

Bill Gertz as President of AIFS oversees the day-to-day operations with close collaboration with myself and the AIFS Inc. Board of Directors.
The current major AIFS activities are as follows:

Study Abroad for U.S. College Students
In affiliation with twenty-four universities in sixteen countries, AIFS organises study abroads annually for more than 5,000 American students during the semester, academic year and summer. Courses are for academic credit. AIFS works closely with 500 American colleges and universities, providing students and faculty with high quality educational experiences abroad.
This division is led by Paul Watson in the US and Mark Simpson and Ailsa Brookes in the UK. Mike DiMauro provides marketing and call centre expertise to this and all other divisions.

American Council for International Studies (ACIS)
ACIS Educational Tours are built on a passionate belief that travel changes lives. Since 1964, ACIS (together with the original AIFS high school programme) has guided teachers and students on over a half million unforgettable study tours. By travelling on an ACIS tour, students gain insight not just from seeing famous places, but also from observing life in and around them. Their commitment to changing lives one by one has made ACIS the most respected name in educational travel, under the leadership of Peter Jones and Becky Tabaczynski.

ACIS Educational Tours
One- to four-week educational tours for teachers and their students to Europe, Asia, Africa, Australia and the Americas comprise the core of ACIS's business. For many participants, an ACIS tour provides their first exposure to a foreign country. Groups stay in three- and four- star hotels, dine on local cuisine, and are

led by highly trained and educated tour managers on visits to sites of cultural and historic significance. To accommodate their educational interests, group leaders are given many opportunities throughout the planning process to customise their tours: they can create a fully-customised tour, customise parts of an existing catalog tour or request a specific commentary from tour managers on a catalog tour. Through their educational tours division, ACIS enables teachers and students from more than 3,000 school districts to travel the world.

Encore Tours

Encore Tours, the performance travel division of ACIS, custom creates performance tours that reflect each ensemble's unique repertoire, experience and interests. Whether they are a choir, orchestra, band, dance troupe or other performing group, Encore's skilled tour consultants create the perfect balance between rehearsals, performances and sightseeing. All Encore Tours are led by highly trained tour managers.

Travel & Company

Travel & Company, the adult travel division of ACIS Educational Tours, understands that travel allows us all, regardless of age, to become students of the world. A Travel & Company tour is more than a visit, it's an exploration.

Camp America

Camp America together with its companion programmes, Campower, brings more than 7,000 international students and young people to the United States each year on official United States Department of State J visas, to work as camp counsellors and support staff in U.S. summer camps.

Camp counsellors teach sports, crafts, performing arts and many other skills to American campers, while Campower participants contribute in the vital areas of maintenance, kitchen and office support. More than 800 U.S. camps participated in 2011, our 45th year of operation. Both programmes are designated by the U.S. Department of State as a J-1 visa sponsor Camp America is led by Dennis Regan in Stamford and Janet Henniker-Talle in London.

> I feel I have grown up a bit, learning important things that will stay with me forever. Seeing kids smile as a consequence of something you have done, is possibly the most rewarding thing.
> Carly Harris, UK Camp America Participant

> The three happy summers I spent with Camp America as a student taught me many things including how to take responsibility for one's life and to get on with people from different backgrounds. These qualities proved invaluable in my career as an explorer and mountaineer.
> David Hempleman-Adams – The first person to walk to both the North and South magnetic and geographic Poles and who has climbed the highest mountains in all seven continents.

Au Pair in America

Au Pair in America places approximately 4,000 eager and skilled young women each year from around the world with American families to care for their children during a mutually rewarding one or two year cultural exchange experience.

Our two Au Pairs have become part of our family and impacted us more than we ever imagined. They have provided loving and caring childcare we never had in regular daycare. Our twins have benefited immensely from their compassion.
Rachelle Holmes, MI Host Parent

Au Pair in America is the live-in childcare solution that meets families' differing needs by offering three programme options:

The standard provides up to forty-five hours of childcare per week.
The Au Pair Extraordinaire also provides forty-five hours of childcare per week. This is for families who seek au pairs who have a formal childcare qualification or two years' full-time experience.
The EduCare in America provides thirty hours of childcare per week. This cost-effective programme is for families with school-age children who require care primarily during the early morning and after-school hours, with some weekend and evening hours.

Au pairs are screened and skilled international young women aged eighteen to twenty-six. Au pairs possess at least 200 hours of prior childcare experience and participate in a comprehensive four-day orientation in the U.S. before being placed with their host family. A local Community Counsellor who provides support for both au pairs and host families and organises social and cultural activities throughout the year, monitors au pairs and host families.

Au Pair in America is officially designated by the U.S. Department of State as a J-1 visa sponsor. Au Pairs are eligible to stay for up to two years on this programme.

This wonderful Au Pair in America has placed more than 80,000 au pairs with host families since 1986. The programme has grown through word of mouth – host families telling friends and neighbours that Au Pair in America provides service, intercultural richness and a reliable source of quality childcare. The US office is led by Ruth Ferry and the UK office by Linda James.

Cultural Insurance Services International (CISI)
Since 1992, Cultural Insurance Services International (CISI) has offered world-class insurance coverage and travel assistance to international travellers. CISI serves both the domestic and international insurance markets and now assists more than 150,000 cultural exchange participants each year on both AIFS and other cultural exchanges.
Among the coverage provided are:

Accident and sickness medical coverage in compliance with U.S. Department of State minimums, with higher limits available;
Accidental death and dismemberment;
Fully assisted medical evacuation and repatriation;
Twenty-four-hour emergency travel assistance;
Trip/programme cancellation coverage;
Tuition reimbursement benefit;
Trip interruption benefits;
Return airfare expense benefit;

Emergency family reunion benefit;

Baggage and personal effects;

Personal liability;

Political evacuation;

Security and risk consulting services;

Comprehensive security benefits to include coverage in the event of natural disasters.

CISI also functions as an authorised Third Party Administrator with a fully automated claim payment system and a staff of professional claim examiners with authority to effect direct payment of claims. Claims are processed promptly and efficiently and can be paid directly to foreign providers in multiple currencies through our London operations centre.

CareMed International Travel Insurance was acquired in 2001 and expands our capacity to offer quality insurance products to international educational and cultural exchange programmes and individuals worldwide. CareMed operates through offices in Germany.

Our expertise in medical, property and liability insurance, as well as travel assistance plans, is unique in the industry. Our relationship with insurance carriers permits us to design comprehensive, cost-efficient coverage.

Both CareMed and CISI specialize in organising insurance plans that meet the needs of its customers for travel abroad on educational and cultural exchanges.

The insurance coverage was originally underwritten by the Insurance Company of the State of Pennsylvania, then known as AIG, with its principal place of business in New York, NY now operating under the brand name of Chartis. However, coverage is now increasingly being underwritten by ACE USA and ACE European Group.

The insurance division is led by Linda Langin.

Independent organisations working closely with AIFS
National Society for the Gifted & Talented (NSGT)

Founded in 2003, NSGT is a not-for-profit 501(c)(3) organisation created to provide recognition and opportunities for gifted and talented children and youth.

As the nation's schools focus on underachieving students, NSGT is dedicated to helping gifted and talented students continue to grow and explore new opportunities. It offers students a certificate of recognition, national resource listings of gifted programmes, discounts on products and services and scholarships to participate in any project/programme related to their educational advancement.

In 2011, NSGT raised scholarship monies from numerous donors including: AIFS Inc., New York Community Trust Foundation, Carmel Hill Foundation, Renaissance Learning, Inc. and York County Community Foundation. The scholarships benefited many recipients from socially disadvantaged backgrounds, enabling 250 students to participate in the Summer Institute for the Gifted (SIG) programme.

In 2009 NSGT became the administrator of the Summer Institute for the Gifted, taking over from AIFS. These programmes are now run on a non-profit basis as a division of NSGT.

Bright, gifted youth are a natural resource that must be cultivated, not neglected. For our country to remain strong, we need the best and brightest to grow to become our future leaders, innovators, and creators. They must be challenged in strong schools; they must be identified and encouraged through the agency of organisations like NSGT, an important force in this task and a needed addition to the efforts to ensure the success of these students who have such great potential.
Patrick Bassett, President National Association for Independent Schools

Summer Institute for the Gifted (SIG)
Founded in 1984 by Phil Zipse and acquired by AIFS in 2000, SIG organises three-week residential and day programmes for approximately 2,500 academically talented young people each year, adding an important enriching supplement to their regular education. SIG blends a strong academic programme of traditional and multidisciplinary courses, an opportunity for cultural exposure, social growth and varied summer camp activities. SIG is now the programme of National Society for the Gifted and Talented, a non-profit 501(c)(3) organisation. SIG is led by Barbara Swicord and Christine Provencher.

The three-week summer residential programmes have a high-quality reputation and are held on the campuses of the following American colleges and universities:

Amherst College, Massachusetts
Bryn Mawr College, Pennsylvania
University of Chicago
Emory University, Georgia
Princeton University, New Jersey
University of California at Berkeley, California
University of California at Los Angeles, California
University of Texas, Austin
Vassar College, New York
Yale University, New Haven, Connecticut

In 2009 a commuter option was added to most residential programmes. In addition, SIG offers three-week day programmes during the summer for students in Kindergarten through grade eight at campuses in California, Connecticut, Florida, Georgia, Massachusetts, New Jersey, New York, Pennsylvania and Washington.

The following organisations have sponsored SIG students in 2011: Carmel Hill Foundation, Edison Schools and Renaissance Learning, with over 200 gifted students from socially disadvantaged areas receiving scholarships.

I was amazed by your programme's organisation, diverse course curriculum and the creative manner in which you motivated and enriched the life of my child this summer.
Maria Norma, NY, Vassar Parent of SIG participant

American Institute for Foreign Study Foundation
Founded in 1967, with the assistance of the late Senator Robert F. Kennedy to help young people from many nations and diverse cultures to understand each other better.

The AIFS Foundation, an independent, not-for-profit, 501(c)(3) tax exempt public charity, provides scholarships to students for participation in study abroad programmes and grants to high schools and institutions to encourage international and educational travel.

The AIFS Foundation also sponsors the Academic Year in America (AYA) programme which enables 1,000 international teenage students to spend a semester or academic year with an American family while attending the local high school. The AIFS Foundation is designated by the U.S. Department of State to issue the J-1 Exchange Visitor Visa for this programme and is the proud sponsor of several U.S. government grant programmes.

Chaired by Ben Davenport, the AIFS Foundation's mission is to provide educational and cultural exchange opportunities to foster greater understanding among the people of the world.

The AIFS Foundation seeks to fulfill its mission by:

Organising high-quality educational programmes at affordable prices enabling young people to live and study abroad;
Supporting educational and travel opportunities for disadvantaged youth;
Developing cooperative programmes between organisations both public and private who share our goals;
Providing grants to individuals for participation in culturally enriching homestay and educational programmes;
The AIFS Foundation is honoured to work with the U.S. Department of State on two prestigious grant programmes;
The Foundation has participated in the Future Leaders Exchange Programme bringing high school scholarship students from the countries of the former Soviet Union to the U.S. to participate in the Academic Year in America programme.

The Foundation is also proud to participate in the YES Youth Exchange and Study programme, which evolved in the aftermath of 11 September, welcoming youth from predominantly Muslim countries to live with American host families and attend high school.

Academic Year in America (AYA)

The Academic Year in America (AYA) programme is one of the most respected high school/homestay programmes in the U.S. Founded in 1981, AYA is well-recognised by high schools across the U.S. and endorsed by thousands of American host families.

Academic Year in America (AYA) is one of the most respected high school/homestay programmes in the United States. Since its founding in 1981, Academic Year in America has enabled more than 30,000 foreign students to come to the U.S. Current annual enrolment is 1,000 students from over thirty-five countries around the world. AYA is well recognized by high schools across the U.S. and endorsed by thousands of American host families. The programme is designated by the U.S. Department of State to issue the J-1 cultural exchange visa and operates in full compliance with programme regulations.

AYA brings international high school students ages fifteen to eighteen and a half to the U.S. to live with carefully screened and selected American host families for a semester or academic year. These young ambassadors attend the local high school and participate in their host families' social and community life. The aim is two-fold:

To develop a greater sensitivity and appreciation of American life on the part of international youngsters, and;
To stimulate Americans' interest in culture and languages other than their own.

The AYA programme is administered by a full-time staff in the main office in Stamford, Connecticut and is supported by a network of over 400 local coordinators across the U.S. who monitor and supervise the students and host families. AYA works cooperatively with international partners from around the world to screen and select the most qualified students for the programme.

> I feel very lucky to be surrounded by so many good people that offer their help when I experience difficulties. Through my studies in high school my English has improved and my knowledge of American history, culture, and traditions as well. I made new friends and improved my socializing skills. Through community service I had the opportunity to play at least a small role in building a new generation based on moral values as I completed 25 hours of community service working with kids between the ages of two and eleven.
> Valentina, student from the Republic of Moldova

> I want to thank you for everything you've done to make my stay in the U.S.A. possible! I am sure I have the greatest host family in the entire country and I'm so happy to be here. I don't even want to go back to Germany.
> Veronica, Student from Germany

The AYA is led by its director, Melanie French.

LIST OF ILLUSTRATIONS